Richard Nixon and Watergate: The Life of the President and the Scandal That Brought Him Down

By Charles River Editors

President Nixon shortly before leaving the White House on August 9, 1974

About Charles River Editors

Charles River Editors provides superior editing and original writing services across the digital publishing industry, with the expertise to create digital content for publishers across a vast range of subject matter. In addition to providing original digital content for third party publishers, we also republish civilization's greatest literary works, bringing them to new generations of readers via ebooks.

Introduction

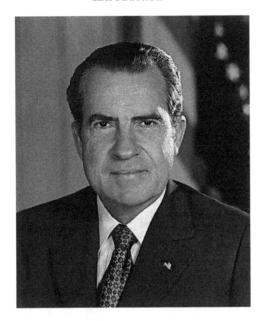

Richard Nixon (1913-1994)

"I leave you gentleman now. You will now write it; you will interpret it; that's your right. But as I leave you I want you to know.... just think how much you're going to be missing. You don't have Nixon to kick around any more..." – Richard Nixon, 1962

A lot of ink has been spilled covering the lives of history's most influential figures, but how much of the forest is lost for the trees? In Charles River Editors' American Legends series, readers can get caught up to speed on the lives of America's most important men and women in the time it takes to finish a commute, while learning interesting facts long forgotten or never known.

Best known as the 37th President of the United States, and the only president in American history to resign his office, Richard Nixon's lengthy political career would put him, during various times, at the center of regional, national and international politics for several decades. It was to be a career filled with unexpected twists and turns, high-profile defeats and unlikely resurrections, in which he made exhaustive efforts to reinvent himself in the public eye. From humble beginnings filled with disparate influences, Nixon's extraordinary intellect, strategic brilliance and imposing style of confrontation saw him through a stellar academic career at Duke

Law School to seats in both the House and Senate, the vice-presidency and finally, the presidency, where he was and is considered by many to be among the strongest foreign policy presidents in the history of the United States. Nixon's presidency is an enigmatic one, given the alternation of previously unimaginable accomplishments in foreign relations, and scandals at home.

With a combative and not wholly scrupulous style of campaigning, or so would say many of his political foes and those of the opposing party, his skills as a prosecutor, coupled with an early decision to ride the existing wave of fear over communism infiltrating the democracy, thrust Nixon into the spotlight as early as 1948. In those early years, he was most famous for his time spent on the House Committee for Un-American Activities, cross-examining suspected Soviet spy Alger Hiss in 1950, resulting in his five-year sentence for perjury

However, when his name was bandied about for vice president on the Eisenhower ticket, Nixon had to worm his way out of serious trouble. America has seen more than its fair share of slick politicians, including those who manage to navigate out of political trouble through charm, but even though Nixon was notorious for not being a warm individual, he managed to orchestrate the infamous "Checkers" speech, which not only saved his political career but effectively worked to force Eisenhower to keep him on the ticket.

Nixon's time as vice president is best remembered for the Kitchen Debate with Soviet premier Nikita Khrushchev, and for the painstakingly close 1960 election against Democrat John F. Kennedy. When Nixon lost that election and then lost the race for California governor in 1962, it seemed his political career was finished. Nixon himself had famously told reporters they wouldn't have Nixon to kick around anymore, but he ended up running for president in the tumultuous year of 1968, with the Vietnam War at its height and political assassinations rocking the country. As it turned out, Nixon edged out Hubert Humphrey to become president, with many crediting it to his "Southern Strategy", but either way, it was an incredible political turnaround for a man whose public career seemed finished 6 years earlier.

Nixon's first term was fruitful in several respects, especially when it came to his favorite issue: foreign policy. In addition to "opening up China" with his historic trip there, Nixon began to wind down American involvement in Vietnam, and along with Henry Kissinger, he set crucial policies for dealing with the Middle East. As President, he held his own with the leadership of Russia and China, thawing relations and increasing trade with Asia, remarking in a later interview that whatever warmth a president might show externally to the public, he wanted a cold president without feeling when there was a difficult decision to be made, or an opposing power to be faced.

By 1972, Nixon appeared to be well on his way to reelection, and sure enough, he enjoyed one of the biggest landslides against George McGovern that year. However, despite the fact that Nixon's reelection seemed a cinch, the seeds of his destruction were being sown in the months leading up to the election. Increasingly and mistakenly viewed as a single scandal within the United States government, what is commonly referred to as the Watergate scandal serves as an overarching term for a series of scandals beginning in 1971 and extending through 1974, although more than any other, it refers to the specific break-in at the Watergate Hotel and office complex in Washington, D.C. The crisis, originating in a secretive battle between the two major political parties, the Nixon White House's paranoia, and the ensuing conflict concerning the release of confidential information to the public, induced senior government officials into committing crimes (most notoriously petty burglary) and coverups for the purposes of character assassination and inter-political espionage. Ultimately, Watergate resulted in the first and only resignation of a sitting American president, but only after Nixon had tried at seemingly every turn to hinder investigations and coverup crimes committed by senior officials in his own administration. Watergate has since become so synonymous with scandal that "gate" is typically added to the end of words associated with scandals even today.

For the last 40 years, President Nixon has been mostly reviled, and understandably, he's ranked among the country's worst presidents, but this view of the President and the Watergate scandal was not and still is not necessarily unanimous. A growing number of Republicans, led by conservatives such as former Nixon speechwriter Pat Buchanan, describe the bringing down of the president as a quasi-coup generated by the press and liberal social forces from within the anti-war movement, which gravitated to the release of information on Vietnam, an increasingly unpopular war, and tapping the widespread campus unrest throughout the country. Paul Johnson, in his book, *Modern Times: A History of the World from the 1920s to the Year 2000*, referred to the whole affair as nothing more than "this Watergate witch hunt." [1]

Richard Nixon and Watergate examines the life and legacy of America's most controversial president, and provides a comprehensive analysis of the country's most famous political scandal. Along with pictures of important people, places, and events, you will learn about Nixon and Watergate like never before, in no time at all.

---

[1] Paul Johnson, "Modern Times: A History of the World from the 1920s to the Year 2000", Harper Collins: 2006

Chapter 1: Nixon's Early Years

Nixon as a toddler

Ironically, for a politician who would later have to battle substantial corruption charges, Richard Milhous Nixon was born January 9, 1913 into a poor family in Yorba Linda, California. In fact, he was raised in dire poverty for many years, and before his parents, Frank and Hanna Nixon, moved to nearby Whittier, he worked on the family's lemon farm, the present site of the Richard Nixon Library and Museum. Richard and most of his other siblings were named after famous kings of England, due in part to his ancestors' Scottish, Irish, and English backgrounds. In his case, the future president was named after Richard the Lionheart.

Nixon's father was a grocer before establishing the small lemon farm, while Hanna Nixon worked as a scrubwoman to pay the medical bills. Hanna was a devoted Quaker who would serve as a deep and lasting influence on her son, who became only the second Quaker to be elected president after Herbert Hoover.

Although reports of abuse from his father are sometimes cited, Nixon never seemed to mention it, and regarding the family's state of poverty, he remarked, "We were poor, but the glory of it was we didn't know it."[2] Within the Nixon family, however, the future president was not unacquainted with tragedy. One of five children, he would lose brothers Harold and Donald in 1925 and 1933, the older brother to tuberculosis. Due to his older brother's tuberculosis, Richard

[2] Biography.com, *Richard Nixon Biography* - www.biography.com/people.richard-nixon-9424076?=2

was prevented from all kinds of outdoor activities by his protective parents.

Left to Right, Miss Mabel Wing, and Donald Nixon, Richard Nixon and Evelyn Williams

A 1916 newspaper picture with Richard second from right. In his memoirs, Nixon explained, "The first time my picture appeared in the paper was in 1916. My mother gave us a nickel each to put in a collection basket for war orphans, and a photographer snapped our picture."

Nixon attended Fullerton High School before transferring to Whittier High, where he finished at the top of his class, and contrary to the public image of the much older, stolid man as president, he excelled at sports, enjoyed the game of football, played the piano and appeared regularly in drama productions, both at the school and in community theater. He was also known as a ferocious debater with an uncanny ability to store and organize detailed information, and many of his class remembered a particularly remarkable oration Nixon delivered on the American constitution. At the same time, young Nixon was also engaged by the age of 14 as a barker for the Slippery Gulch Rodeo, "a cover for illegal gambling rooms in the back."[3]

[3] Edward Jay Epstein, *Agency of Fear, Part II: The Politics of Law and Order, the Education of Richard Nixon* - www.agencyoffear.com

In his senior year, Nixon was offered a full scholarship to Harvard University, but he was unable to both meet the financial expenses of school and travel back to California on a regular basis. Certainly under the influence of his mother, who had hoped that her son would become a missionary, he decided to attend Whittier College, where he excelled in the same fashion as he had in high school, completing his undergraduate years with a history degree.

Nixon in high school

After getting his degree, Nixon attended law school at Duke University, where his persistence in studying earned him the nickname "Iron Butt." During his time at Duke, he was deemed by faculty to have written one of the finest dissertations in the history of his discipline, and he always praised Duke, later claiming, "I always remember that whatever I have done in the past or may do in the future, Duke University is responsible in one way or another.".

Such accomplishments should have led to high connections in major American cities, particularly those of the East Coast, but Nixon never found the way to establish the groundwork for such a rise in the legal field, so he eventually returned to California to join the firm of Wingert and Bewley. All the while, he continued to enjoy performing, and his interests in theater would eventually lead him to meet Thelma Catherine "Pat" Ryan, a local teacher and amateur actress from Ely, Nevada. The two were married in June 1940, and they went on to have two children: Tricia (1946) and Julie (1948).

Pat Nixon

In 1942, the now married lawyer went to Washington to take a lower position in the Roosevelt administration's Office of Price Administration, and it was during these years that his aversion to big government programs deepened. It was apparent that working within a Democratic administration was never a good fit for Nixon. Retrospective studies following the Nixon presidency have investigated his six month stint as a minor bureaucrat with the Roosevelt administration closely, in order to ascertain what caused the shift in his political philosophy. According to the Mazo and Hess account - bearing in mind that their biography was written through the lens of two friends, supporters and staff members - "entering a liberal, he emerged conservative."[4] The event is described in the Mazlish "psychohistory" of Nixon as "semi-traumatic."[5]

After that experience, Nixon decided to join the Navy and serve a two-year stint as a ground aviation officer, working primarily in logistics. Initially reluctant to join the conflict as a Quaker, he managed to secure a spot where he would not see direct action, but he quickly gave in to the urge to participate and subsequently served in the Solomon Islands, Green Islands and New

[4] Bruce Mazlish, "Toward a Psychohistorical Inquiry: The Real Richard Nixon", in The Journal of Interdisciplinary History, Vol. 1 no. 1, Autumn, 1970, p. 55

[5] Bruce Mazlish

Caledonia. Nixon returned with two service stars, and as a Lieutenant Commander.

Chapter 2: Nixon's Congressional Career

"This administration has proved that it is utterly incapable of cleaning out the corruption which has completely eroded it and reestablishing the confidence and faith of the American people in the morality and honesty of their government employees." – Nixon making remarks about the Truman Administration, 1951

Once the war was over, it wasn't long before a group of high-profile Republican political leaders back home urged Nixon to run for a House seat against five-term Democrat, Jerry Voorhis, a Yale-educated liberal with ties to left-wing organizations and a fervent supporter of Roosevelt's New Deal. Accepting the recommendation, the disillusioned government worker attached himself to the growing national sentiment against the far left, particularly against what was perceived as communist infiltration of government, the private sector and the American educational system. As he would in future campaigns, Nixon went all-out to paint his opponent as a communist-leaning liberal, engaging the color pink as a metaphor in an age where communist-oriented citizens were commonly called "pinkos."

In this election, Nixon was helped by the fact that Voorhis had been endorsed by the CIO-PAC, a political labor organization suspected of harboring communists within its membership. He was also affiliated with the National Citizens Political Action Committee. Nixon produced Voorhis' voting record on the second organization, which was not so suspect, and managed to conflate it with the CIO-PAC in efforts to confuse the public. "Nixon knew the difference between the two groups - most of the voters did not."[6] A simple distribution of flyers bearing the high points of the Voorhis voting record was enough to paint him as pro-communist.

In 1946, the strategy worked well enough for him to beat the incumbent with 56% of the vote, beating the incumbent by about 15,000 votes. In hindsight, especially after the Watergate scandal, Voorhis, admittedly one of the most liberal representatives in Congress, found a satisfying irony in believing that it was Richard Nixon who had turned out to be the subversive. Voorhis would elaborate at length on his feelings about Nixon in his book, *The Strange Case of Richard Milhous Nixon*, and he described his opponent as "a ruthless opponent [whose] one cardinal rule of conduct [was] to win, whatever it takes to do it."[7]

---

[6] PBS.org - *Nixon; Early Career* - www.pbs.org
[7] Glen Fowler, *Jerry Voorhis, '48 Nixon Foe,* The New York Times, September 12, 1984.

Voorhis

While it was impressive that Nixon was able to beat an incumbent, especially since he had been a practicing lawyer with virtually no political experience, his victory owed more to general public disfavor with the Democrats. The New Deal was not faring well in the new Congress of 1946, a year in which Republicans regained control of the House of Representatives for the first time in over a decade. To put support for the New Deal in perspective, even the young John F. Kennedy, elected to Congress that same year, sided with Nixon against the program, writing that "Mr. Roosevelt has contributed to the end of capitalism in our own county...through the emphasis he puts on rights rather than responsibilities."[8] Nixon himself would espouse what was then known as a "New Federalism," in which powers are transferred from the federal government to the individual states.

In his first term in the House, Nixon served on the Select Committee on Foreign Aid and visited Europe as part of the Herter Commission to report on the newly installed Marshall Plan. His true fame, however, was rooted in his work with the House Committee on Un-American

---

[8] JFK and Nixon - mu.edu - www.mcadams.posc.mu.edu/progjfk1.htm

Activities, where he led the cross-examination of the alleged Soviet spy Alger Hiss, who had been accused of such by self-proclaimed communist Whittaker Chambers. The Committee was populated by right-wing zealots, decorum was in scarce supply, and "Hiss was everything Nixon despised...wealthy, liberal, educated and handsome."[9] Hiss had graduated from Harvard Law, and worked as a clerk for Supreme Court Justice Oliver Wendell Holmes, worked in the Roosevelt administration for the Agricultural Adjustment Association, and was Head of the Carnegie Endowment for International Peace. Nixon's probe of Hiss amounted to an unceasing hounding and harassment, despite his subject's stubborn denials. Although Hiss was believed at first, and Nixon was cast as the public villain, Chambers produced a State Department document typed on Hiss's typewriter, and he was forced to admit that he knew and had associated with Chambers, the Editor of Time Magazine. The ensuing conviction of Hiss added to the luster of Nixon's anti-communist credentials, and even after the end of the Cold War, the Soviet and U.S. governments agreed that, in fact, Hiss had very likely been guilty of espionage. At the time, however, Nixon was only able to catch Hiss on a charge of perjury, for which he was sentenced to five years of prison.

Hiss

After a few years in the House, Nixon took the next obvious step up for an ambitious young politician. In the election of 1950, he ran for one of California's U.S. Senate seats, this time for a seat held by the departing Democratic incumbent, Sheridan Downey. Standing in his way was another liberal Democrat, Helen Gahagan Douglas, perfectly situated for another anti-communist smear campaign due to her leftward leanings. Downey chose not to face her in the primary and retired, leaving the way open for that kind of campaign.

[9] PBS.org

Nixon campaigning in 1950

Douglas, born in New Jersey, was an actress/singer turned politician after a growing sense of obligation to act on behalf of civil rights. Highly favored by the Roosevelt family, particularly Eleanor, she enjoyed widespread support among African-Americans, Jews and the poor, and for her work on women's rights. This tilted institutional support in California away from her, and it was the *L.A. Times* that made the term "pink lady" stick, capitalizing on the growing anti-communist wave. Despite her public esteem and charisma, Douglas came into the public view from Truman's Fair Deal as much as from Roosevelt's New Deal, and many blamed the Democrats for the fall of China to communism. Unlike most of his political opponents, Nixon could match Douglas' abilities as a speaker, and to her further disadvantage, her political views greatly decreased her sources for fundraising.

Douglas

Not surprisingly, the Nixon forces painted her so vehemently as "pink" that she was immediately thrown on the defensive, where she found herself on the wrong side of the rising "communist scare." Combining the various shades of "red" with Douglas' voting record, Nixon stated publicly that "Douglas was pink right down to her underwear." [10] 1950 was a good year for this kind of campaign, because 1950 saw the beginning of the Korean War, the Soviets testing their first atomic bomb, the Rosenbergs' arrest as spies, and the rise of Wisconsin Senator Joe McCarthy. Combined with Nixon's anti-communist record, she was more than vulnerable, and Nixon decided that it was useless to talk about anything else, since communism was the word on every voter's lips at the time- "It was all people wanted to talk about."[11]

[10] Bruce Mazlish

[11]Greg Mitchell, "When a Woman Dared to Run for the U.S. Senate: Helen Gahagan Douglas vs. Richard Nixon", in *The Nation*, July 27, 2012

Nixon on his station wagon tour in 1950

In the historical view of Nixon's vicious campaign style, it is forgotten that Douglas was no lightweight herself, and she leveled some stinging rhetoric against the Republican that inspired a greater degree of wrath than ever. She famously referred to Nixon as "a demagogue who was selling fear...and nice, unadulterated fascism...a peewee trying to frighten people so that they are too afraid to turn out the light."[12] Through such comments, Douglas had opted to strike at the Nixon camp first, but the assault defined the Republican, anti-communist position. Nixon replied hotly, "I'll castrate her!"[13]

---

[12] American Presidents Blog - *Richard Nixon vs. Helen Gahagan Douglas*, Nov. 14, 2008 - www.american-presidents.org
[13] American Presidents Blog

Although other Democrats suffered the same fate by being on the wrong side of the current fear, the Nixon/Douglas race was "perhaps the most celebrated red-smear campaign of the cold war years."[14] In the end, Nixon won the Senate seat handily, but a small California newspaper, the *Independent Review*, introduced the nickname that would stay with the young Republican throughout his congressional and presidential years: "Tricky Dick."[15]

Chapter 3: Vice President

No sooner had Richard Nixon taken his seat in the Senate than the allure of higher office set in. Once considered a meaningless office, he was thrown into the pool as a possible vice presidential candidate, although the party's nominee for the presidency was as yet undecided itself. In contrast to Eisenhower's suggestion, Nixon was clear that it is "just not possible for a vice president to chart his own course."[16] Still, he saw much potential in the office for gathering support while furthering the president's agenda. In 1951, Nixon set out on a 22 state speaking tour, making it clear to party leadership that he could unite conflicting party factions. "His moderate views on domestic policy also made him popular with more liberal audiences."[17]

Although it seems hard to believe now, many widely assumed that Dwight D. Eisenhower would never be president after he failed to enter politics in 1948. That year, President Truman tried to convince Eisenhower to be his vice president, aware that his unpopularity would be boosted by a war hero every American admired. At the same time, making Eisenhower his vice president would clear Ike's path to the presidency in 1952. When Eisenhower refused the offer, it was widely assumed that Truman would lose to Thomas Dewey, who would then presumably be positioned to be president until 1956, at which point Ike would be 66 years old, too old to be president.

As it turned out, Truman famously won reelection in 1948 by the slimmest of margins over Dewey, meaning the path was clear for Eisenhower to run in 1952 if he so chose. Eisenhower mulled over the decision to run for President for months, even while a Draft Eisenhower Movement had sprung up in an eager effort to encourage his run. Having failed to get Eisenhower to be his Vice President, Truman now suggested Eisenhower should replace him, as a Democrat.

There was one question that remained unresolved: was Eisenhower a Democrat or a Republican? For many, including Truman, the answer was of little importance, and for Eisenhower himself the answer seemed insignificant. But the General needed to decided one way or the other before he could expect to run a successful campaign. Previously, Eisenhower

---

[14] Ingrid Winther Scobie, "Helen Gahagan Douglas: Broadway Star as California Politician", in *California History,* Vol. 66 no. 4, December 12, 1987, Berkeley: UC Press

[15] Nixon Presidential Library and Museum, www.nixon.archives.com

[16] United States Senate

[17] United States Senate

was not much of a partisan or an ideologue. Because of the dominance of the Democratic Party since the beginning of the Great Depression, many suspected he would play it safe and run with the party of Jefferson and Jackson.

Nixon and Eisenhower in 1952

Instead, however, Eisenhower chose the Party of Lincoln. Despite Truman's insistence that he run as a Democrat, Eisenhower thought the party favored too much centralization in government, and he preferred the ideology of the Republican Party. Still, even after choosing a party, Eisenhower had still not decided to run. Previously, there were two separate Draft Eisenhower Movements: one in each party. With his announcement of Republican allegiance, the Democratic Draft Movement died. The Republican one, however, gained steam. Hoping to convince Eisenhower to run, New York Governor Thomas Dewey and Massachusetts Senator Henry Cabot Lodge entered Eisenhower's name into the upcoming New Hampshire Primary without the "candidate's" knowledge. The two were especially eager to nominate Eisenhower, fearing that the ultra conservative Senator Taft of Ohio would win the nomination and sink the party's prospects for decades.

In preparation for the 1952 convention, followers of Taft and Eisenhower created a split in the party, and a number of dark horses entered the race hoping to cause a deadlock at the convention. Nixon was obligated to support Earl Warren, who had thrown his hat in the ring from California, but on the train ride to the convention, he secretly lobbied for Eisenhower. Taft supporters later called this "the great train robbery, claiming that he had sold out Taft and Warren in exchange for the vice presidential nomination."[18]

1952 campaign literature

As it turned out, the presidential candidate whose party affiliation had been up in the air until recently began the campaign with Nixon as the vice presidential candidate. However, Nixon soon became Eisenhower's biggest headache of the campaign. On September 18, two months before the election, *The New York Post* ran the headline "Secret Nixon Fund!" The claim was that the vice presidential candidate had organized a wealth-club to pay his expenses illegally. Nixon openly admitted the fund existed and claimed that it was established in conjunction with his Senate fund, which was (supposedly unbeknownst to him) illegal. If he was actually unaware

---

[18] United States Senate

of that illegality, it was a rare oversight on Nixon's part, but either way, Eisenhower had recently made a publicly overt promise to keep the element of corruption out of Washington, D.C., so the timing was inopportune.

The *Post* and the *Tribune* called for Nixon to withdraw from the ticket, and followers of both Eisenhower and Nixon took up separate sides of the conflict, threatening an already divided Republican Party even further. When Nixon arranged to speak about the issue on national television, former presidential candidate Thomas Dewey advised him that it would be good for the party if he would offer his resignation at that time. When he asked for Nixon's reply, he was told to watch the broadcast with everyone else.

Nixon did not offer his resignation, either privately to Eisenhower, or publicly to the American people. What they received instead was a detailed, exacting account of Nixon's finances, both personal and professional. While Nixon snuck in not so implicit attacks on the Democratic ticket by insinuating his vice presidential counterpart put his wife on the payroll, the speech has been famously dubbed the "Checkers" speech because Nixon told the American public that he intended to keep one campaign gift:

> "That's what we have and that's what we owe. It isn't very much but Pat and I have the satisfaction that every dime that we've got is honestly ours. I should say this—that Pat doesn't have a mink coat. But she does have a respectable Republican cloth coat. And I always tell her that she'd look good in anything...

> One other thing I probably should tell you because if we don't they'll probably be saying this about me too, we did get something-a gift-after the election. A man down in Texas heard Pat on the radio mention the fact that our two youngsters would like to have a dog. And, believe it or not, the day before we left on this campaign trip we got a message from Union Station in Baltimore saying they had a package for us. We went down to get it. You know what it was.

> It was a little cocker spaniel dog in a crate that he'd sent all the way from Texas. Black and white spotted. And our little girl—Tricia, the 6-year old—named it Checkers. And you know, the kids, like all kids, love the dog and I just want to say this right now, that regardless of what they say about it, we're gonna keep it."

In addition to deftly brushing off the attacks on him, Nixon also boxed in Eisenhower by appealing to Republican voters and bigwigs to make his decision for him:

> "I am submitting to the Republican National Committee tonight through this television broadcast the decision which it is theirs to make. Let them decide whether my position on the ticket will help or hurt. And I am going to ask you to help them decide. Wire and write the Republican National Committee whether you

think I should stay on or whether I should get off. And whatever their decision is, I will abide by it.

But just let me say this last word. Regardless of what happens I'm going to continue this fight. I'm going to campaign up and down America until we drive the crooks and the Communists and those that defend them out of Washington."

It was a stroke of political genius, and despite critics such as Walter Lippman, who called it "the most demeaning experience my country has ever had to bear,"[19] and General Lucas Clay's description of it as "corny," Nixon saved his candidacy and advanced the collective ticket in one fell swoop. The message reached average Americans in a way no one could have expected, other than Nixon himself, who patterned the strategy after the famous film *Mr. Smith Goes to Washington*. True to that example, 60 million viewers watched the speech, which resulted in 160,000 telegrams, almost entirely in support. Historian Hal Bochin explained that Americans could identify with the materials of the story—the low-cost apartment, the struggle with the mortgage payment, the parental loans, the lack of life insurance on the wife and children, and even the wife's cloth coat. By reputation, Nixon was a political fighter and also a family man, and the public admired the father who would not give back the family dog 'regardless of what they said about it.'"

The vice presidential candidate all but took the matter out of the former general's hands and entrusted it to the party regulars, and in the end, Eisenhower responded by announcing the vice presidential candidate as his choice to the public. Nixon's entry onto the national ticket was made behind closed doors, but he was in many ways the perfect match: "Eisenhower picked Nixon as his vice presidential nominee in 1952 because he had qualities Ike lacked. The old warhorse from Kansas needed someone young and nakedly political."[20] Eisenhower was concerned in no small measure about his own health, and needed much more than a fill-in or an impotent figure to fill the chair in the worst case. In addition, Nixon "was an internationalist and supported the Marshall Plan,"[21] and he was intensely loyal to the Republican agenda as shaped by his head of the ticket. Through his inclusion, the odds of winning California were greatly improved, and adding his anti-communism strength made the pair all but unassailable on the "red-scare" issue. Nevertheless, the damage Nixon caused created terse relations between him and Ike, which would come back to haunt Nixon in 1960.

Some observers are still surprised that Taft was not the choice of the party, since he was considerably more conservative during the anti-red wave sweeping the country, but the sentiment toward Eisenhower the war hero was almost irresistible, with World War II having ended so recently and with the advent of the rising conflict in Korea. Moreover, by picking an outsider as

[19] United States Senate

[20] Jeffrey Frank, "Dwight Eisenhower and Richard Nixon: The Odd Couple", in *The Economist*, February 2, 2013

[21] U.S. News Opinion, "Eisenhower and Nixon: Secrets of an Unlikely Pair" - www.usnews.com

the presidential candidate, the Eisenhower/Nixon ticket campaigned not so much against the opposing ticket directly but against Truman policies that were blamed by many for causing the fall of China to communism. Despite Nixon's more hawkish nature toward unfolding events in Asia and elsewhere, the odd chemistry of Eisenhower the reluctant soldier and Nixon the attack dog worked to perfection. In the election of 1952, the ticket carried 39 of 48 states, and 55% of the popular vote.

As was necessary considering Eisenhower's ongoing health issues, Nixon did much more than occupy a chair and wait for a call to serve; in fact, "under Eisenhower, [he] made the vice-presidency a visible and important office"[22] by chairing National Security meetings and conducting extensive goodwill tours out of the country to shore up support for American foreign policy. This required a keen instinct for foreign affairs, and the education derived from Nixon's vice-presidency would also serve him well as president. These tours were not all sanitized jaunts to friendly locations either, and Nixon impressed Americans and foreign governments alike by his calm in the face of danger, such as an incident in which he was attacked by a mob in Caracas.

More hypersensitive to foreign conflicts and rivalries than Eisenhower, Nixon was frustrated by the president's lack of action against Soviet incursions into its satellite states to put down cultural and political rebellions. With the successful launching of Sputnik in 1957, Eisenhower seemed not to give it much importance, but Nixon felt the sting of lagging behind in direct competition in the space race with the Soviets, and he translated the achievement into a national sense of humiliation. However, Eisenhower found the perfect venting for Nixon's ire when Joe McCarthy, in the mind of the President, had gone too far. Nixon was the ideal individual to put the Senator in his place, being unafraid to debate or belittle anyone who needed it.

An excellent example of a fearless Nixon, and a precursor to his courageous and forward-thinking actions in later foreign policy, came in 1959. That year, the vice president traveled to the Soviet Union, making him the highest-ranking U.S. official to visit the world's first Communist superpower. Each country had arranged to open an exhibit on its culture and technological advances in a major city of the opposite country; and determined not to allow Sputnik to automatically translate into superiority, the American exhibit included construction of an entire American home, "crammed with labor-saving devices which the U.S. exhibitors claimed any American could afford."[23] The heated exchange that followed, known as the Kitchen Debate, would become a memorable note from the Cold War, during which time little exchange was made between the Americans and Soviets. The Soviets were outpaced in the arena of home technology, and would be for some time, so the ever on-the-offensive Khrushchev rejected the exhibit out of hand, reminding Nixon that the USSR was not interested in personal luxury and had more important things on its mind. An undaunted Nixon cautioned the premier that he "should not be afraid of ideas. After all, you don't know everything."[24] Khrushchev,

[22] The Economist
[23] Andrew Glass, "Nixon and Khrushchev Hold Kitchen Debate, July 24, 1957", in *Politico*, July, 2007

never caught without something to say, shot back, "You don't know anything about communism - except fear of it."[25] To cool the emotional temperature following the debate, Nixon and Khrushchev interjected some humor into the proceeding. Khrushchev suggested a light-hearted thank you to the host of the exhibit for allowing them to use the American home as a debate forum. Nixon, with his typical double-meaning smile, half-heartedly apologized for being a poor host. Most notably, Nixon's visit prompted an invitation to Khrushchev to visit the United States.

Nixon and Khrushchev

That Richard Nixon was perfectly positioned for a run at the White House was not in any way accidental. While remaining loyal to the Eisenhower agenda, he consciously gathered and cultivated support at every turn, and he was even associated at times with the term, "Mr. Republican." The initial phases of his political career, from private life to the House, Senate and the vice-presidency, had all been accomplished in a brief five-year period, and he would serve two full terms in this capacity for Eisenhower, whether the president liked it or not. Indeed, Eisenhower did not always seem happy with the choice.

Roosevelt's first vice president had described the office as "not worth a bucket of warm spit,"[26] and Eisenhower applied the same logic, whether authentically or not, to rid himself of Nixon at least once, hoping to dump him in the beginning and offering him a Cabinet post in the middle of his term with the admonition to Nixon that he only expected to live a few more years. He had suffered heart attacks in 1955 and 1957, so it was not lost on Nixon that while Ike was

---

[24] Politico

[25] Politico

[26] Tom Feran, *Eisenhower and Nixon: Two Terms, but not much Endearment* - Cleveland.com, Feb. 19, 2013

suggesting he shouldn't be wasting his time as vice president, the president also wanted someone else to become president if he did die in office.

Nixon was never part of Eisenhower's inner circle, and outside of the golf course, he was never invited to the White House for social purposes. They only drew closer in later years due to the intermarriage of the families, but even then, it is widely believed that Eisenhower discouraged his grandson David's romance with Julie Nixon. That said, by the time Nixon was president, according to writer Jeffrey Frank, "Eisenhower's feelings for Nixon had changed from 'mild disdain' to 'hesitant respect.'"[27]

Chapter 4: The 1960 Election

The candidates for the 1960 election were not on firm footing with the changing format of presidential politics. The advent of television was strange to both men, and the more transparent nomination system that came into effect some years later did not function in the same way as it does in modern times. This included the use of primaries to test the waters and to practice one's presentation to the public in preparation for later and larger events. The actual decisions were often made by fewer people, and in relative secrecy, in the infamous smoke-filled rooms where party bosses negotiated out of the public eye.

Privately, John F. Kennedy and his father Joe had discussed the 1960 election since Kennedy's Vice Presidential hopes in 1956. John thought his Catholicism was the biggest barrier to the Presidency, while his father thought otherwise. To Joseph Sr., the nation had grown beyond its anti-Catholic sentiments and was ready to accept a Catholic President. Furthermore, since the 1956 Convention, the media had viewed Senator Kennedy as the frontrunner for the Democratic nomination. Polls of Democratic voters confirmed this view, showing Senator Kennedy in a tie with former nominee Adlai Stevenson for the 1960 nomination.

In late 1959, John announced his candidacy for the Presidency of the United States. Members of the Democratic Party elite, however, held reservations. Coming off the popular Eisenhower Presidency, the Democrats felt they had no room to nominate a "risky" candidate. Many still saw John's youth and his Catholicism as liabilities that could give the election to the Republicans in a close race. Other members of the Democratic elite stirred factions of the party against Kennedy. Among the most important anti-Kennedy leaders was Eleanor Roosevelt, who despised Joseph Sr. and thought his son to be too conservative. In part because of Mrs. Roosevelt, liberal Democrats were increasingly deterred from the Kennedy candidacy.

At the start of the campaigning, a poll of Congressional Democrats put John in fourth behind Lyndon Johnson, Adlai Stevenson and Stuart Symington for the nomination. Stevenson had long been a national figure, and Lyndon Johnson was one of the most influential members in

---

[27] Cleveland.com

Congress. Kennedy thus had a difficult campaign on his hands. Winning the nomination would require convincing Democratic liberals of his candidacy (despite his fairly conservative Congressional voting record), ensuring his religion would not be a distraction or a negative, and beating several potentially tough opponents.

Ultimately, the political environment proved ideal for Senator Kennedy to run for president, Throughout the few primaries that were conducted that year, John had the opportunity to prove his broad appeal to the Convention's party elders. His win in the largely white and Protestant state of West Virginia seemed to clinch his claim that he did not just appeal narrowly to fellow Catholics. At the Democratic Convention in Los Angeles, Kennedy won the nomination on the first ballot.

While Kennedy had to field numerous challenges from within his party, and issues of his religion from mainly Protestant America, Nixon was largely unencumbered on the right except for a possible challenge mounted by Nelson Rockefeller. Nixon, however, made some mistakes up front, such as promising to campaign in every state, which required him to spend valuable time in states he could not win, or states with few electoral votes. During the campaign, he would be forced into a two-week hospital stay due to an injury, and despite using his own advertisements as camera practice for the coming debates, he was singularly uninformed of the subtleties required by the medium, despite his rhetorical abilities.

Also potentially working against Nixon was his inability to distinguish himself from Kennedy in the stark ways he had against previous opponents. The wide chasm of modern liberal and conservative stances was nothing like the divide in the 1960s; Nixon, by today's standards, would not be deemed a true conservative, and JFK was far less liberal than the modern voter might think, as he is often mistakenly lumped in ideologically with his brother Ted. Both were pro-civil rights, but JFK's intervention on behalf of Martin Luther King gave him a decided edge. Both were against the FDR New Deal and the welfare system in general. One of their only differences may have been a general tendency on the part of Nixon toward "hawkishness." A common difficulty for both parties was that Nixon and Kennedy were strongly disliked in the south due to their support of the civil rights movement.

At the onset of the campaign, Nixon was favored over Kennedy by a significant margin, and by the summer, his lead stood at around six points. To bolster his candidacy, both among important demographics and to ease doubts about his inexperience, John preferred Senate Majority Leader Lyndon B. Johnson of Texas as his vice president for a variety of reasons. Electorally, he thought Johnson made sense: being from Texas, he could help balance Kennedy's decidedly New England appeal. Additionally, Johnson was much older than the youthful Kennedy, which would help deflect concerns about the candidate's age and inexperience. Of course, in the realm of governing, Johnson was a veteran in Washington, having risen to the position of Senate Majority Leader and becoming one of the most powerful wielders of power in the history of that body.

Johnson's experience would prove critical in governing the nation, as he had the connections and know-how that Kennedy admittedly did not.

Bobby Kennedy, however, was not convinced that Johnson was a good selection. Candidly, Bobby thought Lyndon Johnson was an intellectual lightweight, an accusation tinged with sectionalist prejudices. Bobby, from Massachusetts, thought the Texas Senator was wholly unintelligent, and when John called Johnson to ask him to be the Vice Presidential nominee, Bobby reportedly contacted Johnson to ask that he decline the offer. This accusation has never been confirmed, but it is known that Johnson contacted John again to confirm that he had actually been offered the nomination.

Regardless of what actually occurred, the damage between Bobby and Johnson had been done. Though the personal relationship between the Texas Senator and John was not strained, any semblance of friendship between Bobby and Johnson was over. While this may not have seemed relatively important at the time, when nobody could foresee Vice President Johnson succeeding President Kennedy, the relationship between LBJ and Bobby would play a prominent role in the Election of 1968.

Nixon, on the other hand, selected Henry Cabot Lodge from Massachusetts, in a sense invading Kennedy's strongest territory. And while Nixon did not make a major case of Kennedy's religion, many Protestant ministers did. The only previous Catholic candidate had been Al Smith, who was defeated soundly by the only other Quaker president, Herbert Hoover. Groups for religious freedom contended that Kennedy's Catholicism would make governing the nation as President difficult. Many were suspicious that he would accept demands from the Pope and the Catholic Hierarchy, but by September, Kennedy closed the issue in a speech in Houston, where he said he was running to be a "President who happens to be Catholic," not a "Catholic President." For the remainder of the campaign, Kennedy's religion no longer fascinated the media, though it was likely still privately on the minds of many voters.

Passing on the religious question, "the Republicans portrayed Nixon as the son of a hard-working middle class family and highly experienced world statesman. They portrayed Kennedy as a rich little boy who was more interested in chasing women than meeting his obligations..."[28] Kennedy, on the other hand, viewed Nixon as a "hothead," but he was less successful in making the label stick to his opponent. In selling himself, however, Kennedy did well, and made much of his war record of decorated heroic actions. Nixon countered with his anti-communism credentials, attempting to once more ride the wave of public sentiment against infiltration of public and private institutions by red operatives, but Kennedy couldn't be painted soft on communism either.

In political hindsight, the erasure of Nixon's lead is credited, more than anything else, to the

---

[28] American Political Buttons; Election of 1960 - americanpoliticalbuttons.com

four televised debates held between the two candidates in September and October. Television, although having existed for some time, was still not as much a part of the American political fabric as it would be in later decades, and it was less well understood by political candidates in general. In 1950, television ownership had totaled 10%, but by 1960, the number had risen to 88%.

Nixon negotiated with Kennedy, requesting one debate only in hopes of scoring a "knockout" blow, and as the candidate in the lead at the time, it is unusual that he did not get his way. When Kennedy requested five debates, Nixon was so sure of his superiority in this arena that he agreed to four, the first of which would be entirely devoted to domestic policy, which was certainly not Nixon's strong suit. On September 26, the two met in Chicago, pre-empting the Andy Griffith Show, and Richard Nixon would learn a painful lesson in the subtleties of television. Kennedy, on the other hand, had given the matter more thought and preparation, and "seem[ed] to have been aware of television as a medium."[29]

Despite airing in black and white, the television broadcast showed stark contrasts in shading between the two debaters. Kennedy had recently arrived from Florida, tanned and rested, while Nixon had been in the hospital with a knee injury. Kennedy played well before the camera and appeared comfortable with the format, while Nixon sweated profusely and had not received good counsel on make-up, which made his five o'clock shadow stand out prominently. The Democrat had visited the studio a day before to discuss logistics of the set and camera placement with the producer, so his blue suit made him appear distinct, while Nixon's grey suit tended to absorb him into the background. Perhaps most notably, Nixon undertook a more traditional style of debate, addressing his remarks to his opponent, while Kennedy addressed the cameras directly, and by

[29] Mary Ferrell Foundation - *Kennedy-Nixon Debates* - www.maryferrell.org

doing so, he appeared to address the American people directly.

The general feeling among those of the television audience was that Kennedy was the clear winner of the first debate, and polling data later revealed that Kennedy won three out of four votes cast by those who used the first debate to decide. Among radio listeners, Nixon was deemed the winner based on more detailed and confident content, but by far, the major viewership was through television. The Republican's running mate, Henry Cabot Lodge, was heard to remark after the first debate, "That son of a bitch just lost the election."[30]

The second debate was held in Washington, D.C. on October 7, the third with Kennedy situated in New York and Nixon in Los Angeles on October 13th, and the fourth in New York on October 21, devoted entirely to matters of foreign policy. By this time, however, the damage was done, and Nixon had lost the lead he had held since the beginning of the campaign almost overnight.

Also hurting Nixon's cause was the lack of campaigning done by the president on his behalf, despite the fact Ike was still popular. As 1960 approached, the fact that Eisenhower/Nixon had been an arranged political marriage became all the more clear, and overlapping theories abound as to why Eisenhower did not show more eagerness in attempting to put his vice president over the top. Various off-hand remarks by the outgoing president hurt Nixon personally and professionally, in particular a press conference at which Eisenhower was asked if his vice president had ever had one single idea of merit. Eisenhower answered, "If you give me a week, I'll think of one. I don't remember."[31] Frank adds that Eisenhower "instantly regretted the remark, but didn't rush to clarify it."[32]

Overall, Nixon experienced Eisenhower in an entirely different way from the public perception, and he came to believe Ike was cold, calculating and occasionally cruel. Either way, it was widely noted that the president only became engaged in Nixon's campaign during its final 8 days. Certainly, Nixon wanted to be seen as his own man, and in Eisenhower's defense, he had expressed a desire to do a great deal more for the new Republican ticket. Mamie Eisenhower, however, confided to Pat Nixon that her husband's fragile health would be further endangered if he took the suggested campaign swing through several states in a whirlwind timetable. Eisenhower was never informed of the first lady's communications with Mrs. Nixon, and thus never understood why he wasn't called. Nixon was also pressed by Maj. General Howard Snyder, the president's physician, to avoid allowing Eisenhower to campaign in any ongoing capacity, even though Eisenhower was "raring to go."[33]

---

[30] Mary Ferrell Foundation

[31] Cleveland.com

[32] John H. Taylor, *Eisenhower and the 1960 Election - The New Nixon*, September 23, 2008

[33] John H. Taylor, *Eisenhower and the 1960 Election*

After the debates, Kennedy spent the remaining time patching together a viable Election Day coalition. African-Americans were an important piece of the Democratic coalition, but Kennedy's past hesitance on civil rights issues put that voting bloc in jeopardy. He decided to risk losing Southern white segregationists by coming out more loudly in support of civil rights, which eventually won him the endorsement of Martin Luther King Jr.

By November, the gap between the two candidates was paper thin. Kennedy remained strong among "white ethnics," labor and African-Americans, while Nixon appealed to rural Protestants, the West Coast, and parts of the South. On Election Day, the popular vote was as close as polls suggested: Kennedy won by a hair, with 49.7% to Nixon's 49.5%. The Electoral College vote, however, was a different story, with Kennedy winning with 303 votes to Nixon's 219. In Mississippi, eight unpledged delegates went to Strom Thurmond and Harry Byrd, one to Byrd and one to Goldwater in Oklahoma, and six for Byrd in Alabama.

During election night, several races had maintained a tensely close margin in the voting. Kennedy was thought to have won California late into the night, but this was reversed by an influx of absentee votes. By the same token, Nixon appeared to have won Hawaii, a count that was soon reversed. Nixon's friend, Earl Mazo, who would later co-author one of his biographies, published a series of articles detailing the irregularities in the voting nationally, not providing any margin for precincts in which voting machines were used, generally controlled by the Republicans.

Reports of outright frauds were particularly centered around Democratic machine politics in Cook County, Illinois and in the state of Texas. In Illinois, Kennedy prevailed by a margin of only 8,858 votes, and due to the "unsavory reputation of the Chicago Democratic Organization and newspaper reports,"[34] the entire Republican Party was certain that the presidency had been stolen from their man. The question in Illinois came down to two Cook County precincts in which ballots were completed by hand. Ordinarily, there was no provision for a presidential recount unless other races met the qualification of certain percentage of one candidate's votes going missing, or being found on the other's ledger. This occurred, and a "discovery recount" was undertaken, with the suspicion that although Nixon would probably gain votes, the improvement would not be as prodigious as with some of the other Republican candidates.

From the beginning of the ordered recount, the Democrats, led by the Daly machine, dragged the pace to a crawl, to the point that County Judge Thaddeus Adesko ordered additional panels of vote counters to join the recount, which was finally completed on December 9th. The results demonstrated "that the counting of the paper ballots in Chicago had been unbelievably sloppy and inaccurate...[showing] gross errors in which the miscount led to a net shift of fifty votes or more."[35] This did not prove beyond the shadow of a doubt that Nixon would have won Illinois,

[34] Edmund F. Kallina, "Was the 1960 Presidential Election Stolen? The Case of Illinois", in *Presidential Studies Quarterly*, Vol. 15 no. 1, Winter 1985

but the Republicans inevitably argued with the recount as well, and may have been right in doing so. Naturally, those who knew Nixon best claimed that the defeated candidate was certain beyond any doubt that the election had been stolen until the day he died. Nixon was praised for refusing to join in with the voices that called for a federal investigation and the filing of lawsuits in Illinois and Texas, due to what he described as the fear of a constitutional crisis, but in the following decades it was made clear how much his surrogates actually tried to overturn the results.

Regardless, John F. Kennedy had just become the youngest man ever elected President, and the first Roman Catholic. He was sworn in as the 35th President of the United States on January 20, 1961. Despite heavy snow, the festivities surrounding Kennedy's inauguration were exciting. President Kennedy attended Mass at the Holy Trinity Catholic Church in Georgetown, a gesture that greatly pleased his fellow Catholic Americans, who were thrilled to have a President "of their own." And of course, most famously, in his inaugural address he asked Americans to "ask not what your country can do for you, but ask what you can do for your country."

Chapter 5: The Wilderness Years and 1968 Election

Returning to California, Nixon had no further plans for political campaigns, intending to disappear from public life and lick his wounds. However, as had occurred before his first House race, a group of California political "high rollers" convinced him "that he needed to run [for the office of Governor of California] to remain politically viable."[36] Nixon unadvisedly accepted the challenge. At one point during the campaign, Nixon was considered to be doing very well by hitting his opponent for being soft on crime and communism, familiar themes for a Nixon campaign. However, Pat Brown countered that Nixon was not the slightest bit interested in being the Governor of California, and that his only interest in the state was as a stepping stone to the White House.

What turned the tide in the California election, despite the mid-campaign gains made by Nixon, was the Cuban Missile Crisis, a showdown between the American and Russian leadership that thrust Kennedy into the limelight. The perception of his successful handling of the crisis raised the stock of Democratic candidates and incumbents everywhere, including that of Pat Brown. In the two weeks of Kennedy's crisis with Khrushchev and the Soviet Union, Nixon realized that such an historical event going the Democrat's way would spell the end of his campaign in California.

Sure enough, Nixon would go on to suffer his second major defeat in a two-year period, this time by over 300,000 votes, and with that, he was generally thought to be finished for good in high level politics. The end came with a famous press conference in which Nixon bitterly and

---

[35] Edmund F. Kallina

[36] Los Angeles Times, *Looking Back at the 1962 Gubernatorial Race - Debate: Former Governor Edmund G. (Pat) Brown and ex-president's former campaign manager discuss the election at Richard Nixon Library and Birthplace,* March 22, 1992

sarcastically stated, "I leave you gentleman now. You will now write it; you will interpret it; that's your right. But as I leave you I want you to know.... just think how much you're going to be missing. You don't have Nixon to kick around any more, because, gentlemen, this is my last press conference, and I hope that what I have said today will at least make television, radio, the press recognize that they have a right and a responsibility, if they're against a candidate give him the shaft, but also recognize if they give him the shaft, put one lonely reporter on the campaign who'll report what the candidate says now and then. Thank you, gentlemen, and good day."

In a taped phone conversation released many years later, President Kennedy and Pat Brown were heard discussing Nixon's mental state, and the tone of the call suggests that Kennedy gave Brown personal and specific advice on how to defeat Nixon. Brown responded that he had followed instructions as given, and during the call, the President was heard to say, "You reduced him to the nut house...that last farewell speech of his...it shows that he belongs on the couch."[37] Unaware that he was being recorded, Brown went on to say, "This is a very peculiar man. I really think that he is a psycho. He's an able man, but he's nuts."[38]

Nixon himself described the following period of time as his "wilderness years", and in a retrospective held at the Nixon Library between former California Governor Pat Brown and Nixon's campaign manager, H.R. Haldeman, the future Republican aide for Nixon at the White House, remarked that he believed the loss to be a good thing, and that "because of the loss, Nixon was far better prepared for, and more ready to serve as President of the United States...if Nixon had become governor, the course of history would have been radically different."[39]

How Richard Nixon accomplished such a complete resurrection as a central figure of national politics is still viewed as a historical wonder, especially following two such bitter defeats at the national and state level. However, the drive to stay relevant within the picture of his party, and an uncanny gift for reinventing himself brought Nixon back from the political dead. By 1967, he was declaring his intentions to run for the presidency again, despite his wife Pat's misgivings.

At the same time, none of this occurred within a vacuum. Following his defeat in California, he joined a prestigious law firm in New York, argued a case before the Supreme Court, wrote a best-seller entitled *Six Crises*,[40] and toured Europe, meeting with foreign leaders. Campaigning tirelessly for fellow Republican candidates around the country, he began to assemble a network of support, and the nickname of "Mr. Republican" became more of a national catch-phrase among party members than ever.

For the election of 1968, several circumstances tended toward a Nixon advantage. First, the available challengers in the Republican Party were, for one reason or another, not suited to serve

[37] Christopher Matthews, *Former Governor Called Nixon 'Psycho'* - SFGate
[38] Christopher Matthews, SFGate
[39] Los Angeles Times
[40] Nixon Library and Museum - www.nixonlibrary.org

as party frontrunners. George Romney enjoyed a brief time as an anti-war candidate, but that constituency could not sustain him on the national stage, and his comment about being "brainwashed" on Vietnam did him in politically. Barry Goldwater had already been hopelessly defeated by President Johnson in 1964, and the "new conservative star,"[41] Ronald Reagan, had never yet held public office. Reagan was obligated to try his hand at the state level by first running for the governorship of California. Liberals of the party generally lined up behind Nelson Rockefeller, but they were not a strong faction that year, especially with the troubles facing the Democrats.

Nixon had not really made his move yet, but he was immediately aided in his vault to the front by Lyndon Johnson's comment that Nixon was a "chronic campaigner."[42] In a way that the Democrats could not hope to demonstrate in 1968, the Republican Convention was a display of congeniality and unity, despite the various factions supporting a separate candidate each. Choosing Marylander Spiro Agnew as his running mate, Nixon won the nomination on the first ballot, with Reagan moving to make it unanimous. Conservatives such as Goldwater and Thurmond immediately joined in the support. From that moment, the results of Nixon's work since the 1962 defeat took effect, and he demonstrated himself to be a far more thoughtful and careful candidate than in the past. The image of a "New Nixon" emerged, "more statesmanlike, less combative , more mature and presidential."[43] He refused to debate the Democratic candidate at all, rather than walk into any sort of ambush as he had in 1960, and given that he enjoyed a double-digit lead at the time, he saw no reason to risk it.

The Democrats, on the other hand, were in terrible disarray. The Vietnam War raged with no honorable end in sight. President Kennedy had been assassinated several years before, and public unrest at home grew by the day. Even still, when Senator Eugene McCarthy decided to throw his hat into the ring, it was a surprise, but it was an even greater one when he was only narrowly defeated in the first primary in New Hampshire on March 12th. Though Johnson had won the primary, the close margin made him appear vulnerable, an unusual position for a sitting president, and after McCarthy's close shave in New Hampshire, Bobby Kennedy judged the time was right to enter the race. With "Camelot" still fresh in America's minds, he declared his candidacy for the Presidency of the United States, and Bobby announced his candidacy from the same location where his brother had announced his own 8 years earlier: the Russell Senate Office Building in Washington. The McCarthy campaign charged that he was an opportunist, relying on McCarthy's initial candidacy before declaring its own, but regardless, the Kennedy name continued to attract Americans across the country, and Bobby represented another chance at Camelot.

Kennedy's candidacy, as well as McCarthy's, indicated the deep division within the

---

[41] Miller Center - *Richard M. Nixon* - www.millercenter.org.
[42] Miller Center
[43] Miller Center

Democratic Party over the Vietnam War. On the one side was President Johnson, while Kennedy and McCarthy together split the anti-war vote. The pro-war Democrats ultimately lost their leader on March 31st, when President Johnson made an historic move and announced he would no longer seek reelection. Johnson was consumed by the Vietnam War while in the White House, and he had little time to campaign; in fact, he never left the White House during the New Hampshire campaign, and he feared that a long and brutal primary campaign, along with an equally onerous general election campaign, would sink his Presidency and his chances of winning.

President Johnson

Kennedy seemed to be on the rise during the summer, only to be assassinated by Sirhan Sirhan on the night he won the California primary. At this point, Hubert Humphrey, the former vice president, joined in the race. The anti-war faction did not fully line up behind McCarthy as expected, and Humphrey won the nomination in one of the ugliest convention displays in the annals of American history, choosing Maine's Edmund Muskie as his running mate. Police intervention on the convention floor and the subsequent large-scale violence experienced on live television from Chicago left the Democratic party shattered and running from far behind. In an additional twist, Alabaman George Wallace mounted a national campaign as the candidate for the American Independent Party, receiving significant support in the Deep South.

Through all of this, Nixon remained steady, ensuring he was portrayed "as a figure of stability in a time of national upheaval. Nixon promised a return to traditional values and 'law and order.'"[44] Nixon's alleged "Southern strategy," which challenged Democratic liberals to more openly defend their liberal positions, was intended to capture the entire south for the Republican

---

[44] Nixon Presidential Library & Museum

Party in a lasting voting bloc, which if true, was a successful gambit on Nixon's part. Some refute the notion of such a strategy, however, or at least of its abiding success, reminding us that "the growth of GOP support among white southerners was mostly steady and mostly gradual from 1928 to 2010."[45] Perhaps most notoriously, Nixon scuttled peace talks to end the Vietnam War until after he was elected.

In winning the 1968 election by a popular margin of almost half a million votes (but in an electoral landslide), Nixon had abandoned the one-trick strategy of anti-communism and replaced it with a plan to withdraw from Vietnam without the country appearing to be weak, promises to restore law and order to a society in chaos, and to represent what he termed the "great silent majority."[46]

Chapter 6: Nixon's Shadow Government and First Term

Nixon being sworn in

The realization that Nixon was reticent to allow for a wide distribution of power within the executive branch became apparent almost immediately after he took office, and it is said that his "predilection for secrecy and intrigue"[47] served as a logical base for his love of executive privilege and general unaccountability in the office of the presidency by collegial institutions of

[45] Dan McLaughlin, *The Southern Strategy Myth and the Lost Majority: How Republicans Really Lost the South,* Red State, Jan. 11, 2014
[46] Nixon Presidential Library & Museum
[47] Len Colodny, Robert Gettlin, *Silent Coup,* St. Martin's Press: New York, 1991, p. 93

government. Despite the public image he had attempted to craft, the new president arrived to the White House still harboring bitter feelings toward those who had prevented his early election, and at those he felt had not properly respected him during the vice-presidency. He still felt the exclusionary sentiment of the East Coast establishment, the "Harvardians," the wealthy and the famous. According to sources close to the presidency, Nixon would frequently "despair at his lack of charisma,"[48] strengthening the urge in him to fight back whenever slighted, and to neutralize all forms of opposition through stealth and sophisticated institutional maneuvering. In such a mindset, this "intensely private and withdrawn man"[49] established what many later referred to as a "secret government" that did not in the least offend his view of correct procedure in the face of prevailing circumstances.

Nixon's underlying conviction held that the Federal Bureau of Investigation was an agency to be used freely by the president, and he was astonished that Director J. Edgar Hoover would not readily comply to all of his requests. During his first term, Nixon actually went outside government agencies to hire a detective agency that would do the things that the FBI would not. The individual of choice was John Caulfield, a highly experienced New York agent who suggested that he join the White House Staff instead of working each project as an independent contractor under the table. Investigations of alleged enemies and political rivals were legion, including George Wallace, Hubert Humphrey and Edmund Muskie. On top of that, Nixon ordered the investigations of anti-war groups, various entertainers and, at times, members of his own family. For example, Nixon kept tabs on his nephew Donald Nixon Jr., whose entry into a potentially embarrassing business venture brought Washington scrutiny, and when Julie Nixon was said to have received a teaching job too easily, those who questioned her application were investigated. On more than one occasion, Nixon requested 24 hour surveillance on Senators who openly disagreed with him on the Senate floor or in the press, and almost all forms of entertainment satirizing the White House during these years met with the same treatment, such as the film *Milhous* (though Nixon himself was not above a high ratings "sock it to me" appearance on the show Laugh-In).

A second alternative to the FBI and other federal agencies was found through the use of the National Security Council, an organization that had remained fairly inactive throughout the previous two administrations. Its members were in large part officers of the Cabinet and were thus presidential appointments free from Congressional approval. Cabinet members themselves were chosen to be individuals who, in cases of need, could be largely ignored or rolled over. Secretary of State William Rogers possessed a sparse background for the position and was passed over in almost all actions dealing with foreign nations, often being informed after the fact. In the case of Secretary of Defense Melvin Laird, whose experience was significant, a backchannel to the Pentagon was created as a detour around his office. The Pentagon was encouraged by Nixon's willingness to use military force, even though it was not really central to

---

[48] Len Colodny, Robert Grettlin, p. 93
[49] Len Colodny, Robert Gettlin, p. 93

his foreign policy views, preferring "diplomacy over confrontation and a continued arms race."[50] At any rate, his willingness to reach out without interruptions of protocol was internally accepted if not outright hailed.

The first years of the Nixon administration were fittingly dynamic, as Nixon himself wasted no time in becoming proactive. He began a phased withdrawal of troops from Vietnam and sought a ceasefire with North Vietnam. A ceasefire was eventually fashioned with Le Duc Tho of the North, but when the South demanded that the document receive major alterations, the North published it. Feeling that the North had attempted to embarrass him, Nixon commenced saturation bombing on cities and supply routes in Cambodia and Laos by December 1969. The action has not-so-affectionately been called "the madman theory," but Nixon believed that he held a winning hand, and he pressed hard for points at the negotiating table and for international respect for American foreign policy. A peace accord was eventually signed in January of 1973, but South Vietnam fell to the North after the complete withdrawal of American troops and the cutting off of all foreign aid by Congress. Ironically, it had been Nixon himself who first proposed sending troops to Vietnam in 1954, only for the idea to be rejected by Eisenhower. In the later conflict, he was also the first senior official in government to consider and possibly recommend the use of nuclear weapons as part of a proposed "Operation Vulture." In this case, Henry Kissinger rejected the idea, but the conversation over nuclear deployment was a serious one, as heard on the later White House tapes.

At the same time, Nixon eased Cold War tensions with the Soviet Union through the second and more successful round of SALT (Strategic Arms Limitation Treaty) Talks, which was eminently more fruitful than any of the Johnson administration's attempts. The first series of SALT talks, initiated by Johnson, had been a bust for the most part, but on the day Nixon took office for his first term, the Soviet Ministry announced its serious interest in continuing negotiations. By October 1969, the White House had secured a round of negotiations to be conducted in Helsinki. This was in America's interest, as Russia had stockpiled an advantage in nuclear weaponry, while the U.S. had remained at approximately the same level since 1967. A second round, resulting in an accord, was held in Vienna in 1972, and Nixon and Brezhnev signed another missile treaty in Moscow that year.

---

[50] Len Colodny, Robert Gettlin, p. 5

Nixon meeting with Brezhnev

The most iconic moment of the Nixon presidency was his trip to China in February 1972, greatly credited with "opening up China". Nixon explained one of the motives for his historic trip: "I had long believed that an indispensable element of any successful peace initiative in Vietnam was to enlist, if possible, the help of the Soviets and the Chinese. Though rapprochement with China and détente with the Soviet Union were ends in themselves, I also considered them possible means to hasten the end of the war. At worst, Hanoi was bound to feel less confident if Washington was dealing with Moscow and Beijing. At best, if the two major Communist powers decided that they had bigger fish to fry, Hanoi would be pressured into negotiating a settlement we could accept." Subsequent U.S. Ambassador to China Winston Lord went further, explaining:

> "First, an opening to China would give us more flexibility on the world scene generally. We wouldn't just be dealing with Moscow. We could deal with Eastern Europe, of course, and we could deal with China, because the former Communist Bloc was no longer a bloc. Kissinger wanted more flexibility, generally. Secondly, by opening relations with China we would catch Russia's attention and get more leverage on them through playing this obvious, China card. The idea would be to improve relations with Moscow, hoping to stir a little bit of its paranoia by dealing

with China, never getting so engaged with China that we would turn Russia into a hostile enemy but enough to get the attention of the Russians. This effort, in fact, worked dramatically after Kissinger's secret trip to China.

Thirdly, Kissinger and Nixon wanted to get help in resolving the Vietnam War. By dealing with Russia and with China we hoped to put pressure on Hanoi to negotiate seriously. At a maximum, we tried to get Russia and China to slow down the provision of aid to North Vietnam somewhat. More realistically and at a minimum, we sought to persuade Russia and China to encourage Hanoi to make a deal with the United States and give Hanoi a sense of isolation because their two, big patrons were dealing with us. Indeed, by their willingness to engage in summit meetings with us, with Nixon going to China in February, 1972, and to Moscow in May, 1972, the Russians and Chinese were beginning to place a higher priority on their bilateral relations with us than on their dealings with their friends in Hanoi."

Nixon and Mao in China

Of course, Nixon attempted to script the trip to appeal to Americans back home, and in televised remarks, he told the nation, "This was the week that changed the world, as what we have said in that Communique is not nearly as important as what we will do in the years ahead to build a bridge across 16,000 miles and 22 years of hostilities which have divided us in the past. And what we have said today is that we shall build that bridge."

Meanwhile, at home, Nixon dismantled much of Lyndon Johnson's work with social and economic programs, vetoing initiatives on health, education and the welfare system. He fearlessly took over congressional funds that he considered ill-spent, over Congressional protests. At the same time, Nixon remained a fanatic for electoral politics, and he fought long and hard for the increased elections of Republican candidates, as well as attempting to gain new territory for the party in state and regional elections. However, in terms of the daily work in Washington, such as dismantling major aspects of the Republican National Committee for fear of them interfering with White House outreach, "Nixon gained a poor reputation...for his work as leader of the Republican Party."[51] In campaigning terms, he was a generous extravert but prone to consolidating and centralizing power to himself, severely crippling traditional party mechanisms.

Chapter 7: The Pentagon Papers, CREEP, and the First Burglaries

"The main further question is the extent to which we should add elements to the above actions that would tend deliberately to provoke a [North Vietnamese] reaction, and consequent retaliation by us.

Examples of actions to be considered would be running US naval patrols increasingly close to the North Vietnamese coast and/or associating them with 34A operations.

We believe such deliberately provocative elements should not be added in the immediate future while the GVN is still struggling to its feet. By early October, however, we may recommend such actions depending on [South Vietnam's] progress and Communist reaction in the meantime, especially to US naval patrols.." – The Pentagon Papers

Mistrust of government was certainly not a new phenomenon when Nixon won the election of 1968 against an opposing Congress for the first time in over a century, but a new culture of secrecy and retaliation would further sour the public's perception of national leadership in the long-term. The psyche of the Nixon White House, as it has come to be better understood, was intricate and calculating. On the night of the 1968 victory celebration, Nixon was said to be "clouded by his reference to the problems of an unsettled war in Vietnam." And yet, it is said that he had scuttled South Vietnam's final hours at the Paris Peace Talks in an effort to stall the resolution until he could be elected. Speaking with the South Vietnamese, and allegedly promising a better deal than they would receive from Humphrey, the delegation vacated the negotiating table until after the election.

---

[51] Robert Mason, "Majority: Richard Nixon as Party Leader, '69-'73: I Was Going to Build a New Republican Party and a New Majority", in Journal of American Studies. British Association for American Studies 50th Anniversary Vol. 38 no. 3, p. 464

Although Watergate is named after the complex that housed the Democratic National Committee in 1972, and the attempted burglary of the DNC offices is often considered the first incident leading to the scandal, Watergate truly had its roots in Daniel Ellsberg's leak of the Pentagon Papers to the *New York Times* in 1971. The Pentagon Papers outlined the course of American intervention in Vietnam, and that summer, the *New York Times* released a series of articles about the papers under the headline "Vietnam Archive: Pentagon Study Traces Three Decades of Growing U.S. Involvement". Coming near the height of the Vietnam War's unpopularity, the leak of the Pentagon Papers badly damaged public morale, and the Nixon Administration sought an injunction to prevent the *Times* from disclosing the previously confidential information. When the *Times* appealed that injunction, it led to *New York Times Co. v. United States*, a suit that quickly reached the Supreme Court.

Ellsberg

Meanwhile, Ellsberg also disclosed information from the Pentagon Papers to the Washington Post, which also began to run stories, and this time, a federal judge refused the request for an injunction, writing, "The security of the Nation is not at the ramparts alone. Security also lies in the value of our free institutions. A cantankerous press, an obstinate press, an ubiquitous press must be suffered by those in authority in order to preserve the even greater values of freedom of expression and the right of the people to know." The government's appeal of that decision led to that case being brought before the Supreme Court along with the *New York Times* case. On June 30, 1971, the Supreme Court ruled in favor of the papers, holding that the government failed to meet its burden of proof for upholding an injunction against the release of the information.

Although the Pentagon Papers mostly covered the Kennedy and Johnson Administration, they were deemed embarrassing enough for the Nixon Administration, as asserted on one tape by Nixon's chief of staff, H.R. Haldeman: "[Donald] Rumsfeld was making this point this morning... To the ordinary guy, all this is a bunch of gobbledygook. But out of the gobbledygook comes a very clear thing.... It shows that people do things the president wants to do even though it's wrong, and the president can be wrong." Nixon's bent for secrecy was brought to full flower by Ellsberg's leaks of classified materials on the Vietnam War, especially when the federal government unsuccessfully fought Ellsberg on every front to prevent or diminish the impact of the Pentagon Papers' publication. In the wake of the Supreme Court decision, the Nixon Administration aimed to punish Ellsberg for what the president saw as an act of treason, and this led to the first noteworthy White House related burglary: an attempt to obtain damaging personal material against Ellsberg in the office of his Washington psychiatrist.

Haldeman

The Nixon administration's response to what it saw as a clear case of treason was to dub such forces as "counter-government," particularly those who supported the publication of the Pentagon Papers in the *New York Times*. As such, the Administration decided to counter Ellsberg and future leaks by forming a "special investigations unit," which would come to be known in time as the "plumbers." The principal figures of this unit included John Ehrlichman, John Paisley (liaison to the CIA), and E. Howard Hunt, a former top-level CIA agent.

At the head of the operation was Nixon's own chief of staff, Haldeman, who served as both recruiter and gatekeeper, once describing himself as "the president's son-of-a-bitch." The entire operation was carried out under the umbrella of the Committee to Re-elect the President, which would later be derisively referred to as CREEP. Gordon Liddy, who would become one of the most high-profile figures in the operation, was recruited by White House Counsel John Dean as a general intelligence gatherer. The crux of the unit's activities was to "harass Nixon's opponents...with wiretaps, burglaries and intercepted mail." The FBI was discouraged from getting near the incident through the White House suggestion that the break-in was a national security operation executed by the CIA.

Hunt

Ehrlichman

Dean, a precocious 32 year old Georgetown graduate, was appointed to White House Counsel after early reviews from his employer raving about his intelligence and skill. "As Watergate broke...[he was] to control the fall out after the burglars were arrested, which involved paying them large sums of money." Dean handled it well, and Nixon applauded, noting to Haldeman that the young lawyer was "a pretty good gem."[52]

According to the White House tapes, Nixon authorized a smear campaign against Ellsberg in July 1971. With that, an agenda of harassments began against Nixon opponents, and though several were canceled before they were attempted, the most noteworthy was not. Hunt personally investigated Ted Kennedy's Chappaquiddick scandal and any potential Kennedy involvement in the assassination of South Vietnamese leader Ngo Dinh Diem, but before the Watergate burglary, the plumbers' most important activity was the September 1971 burglary of Ellsberg's psychiatrist's office. The office's files were ransacked in an attempt for the Nixon Administration to obtain confidential information on Ellsberg, but the burglary, described in Ehrlichman's notes as "Hunt/Liddy Special Project No. 1", failed to turn up Ellsberg's files. Hunt and Liddy then suggested breaking into Ellsberg's psychiatrist's home, but that attempt was never made after Ehrlichman shot it down.

In taking these measures, Nixon's strategy relied on past experience, notably his prosecution of Alger Hiss in 1950. Nixon intended to try Ellsberg through the press, believing that the Justice Department would not follow through, and he boasted on the notorious presidential tapes of the

[52] NBClearn - John Dean Testifies Before Watergate Committee - www.nbclearn.com/portal/site/k-12/flatview?cuecard=72

leaks he had initiated in the earlier Hiss case. Just as the Justice Department dragged its feet in 1950 (at least according to Nixon), the same was true of the FBI in 1971, because Director J. Edgar Hoover refused to authorize an investigation of Ellsberg. As the *Washington Post*'s famous confidential source, "Deep Throat", later explained, "The problem was that the FBI wouldn't burglarize."

Though it wouldn't be revealed for several decades, Deep Throat was Deputy Director of the FBI Mark Felt. As second-in-command at the FBI, Felt had come to Washington to work in the offices of Senator Pope from Idaho, and as a graduate of the George Washington Law School, he held positions at the Federal Trade Commission and other agencies as well. Trained in espionage at the Academy in Quantico, he spent time in the West dealing with organized crime. As a high-ranking member of the FBI, and following the Death of J. Edgar Hoover, Felt had access to literally every scrap of material on the Watergate affair. As Deep Throat, he funneled a constant flow of information and confirmed certain suspicions to the *Washington Post*, and Nixon himself even suspected Felt, saying on tape that he was most likely an informer. As Woodward recalled, "The FBI was battling for its independence against the Nixon administration. Felt was a dashing gray-haired figure...and his experience as an anti-Nazi spy hunter...endowed him with a whole bag of counterintelligence tricks."

Felt

Felt's role as Deep Throat also came about in part due to Nixon's campaign against Ellsberg. With the administration attempting to pull in the FBI as a tool of the presidency rather than as an independently functioning investigative body, a natural resentment added to Felt's circumstantial motivation to assume the role he did. By drawing the FBI closer under his own direction, Nixon was trying to alter the body that would ordinarily investigate the federal government into a weapon with which to harass and illegally investigate others. Felt took this to heart as deeply as anyone in the Bureau, and "was so wounded that he was passed over for the top job, furious at Nixon's choice of an outsider...and determined that the White House not be allowed to steer and stall the Bureau's Watergate investigation, [that he] slipped into the role that would forever alter his life."[53]

While the burglary of Ellsberg's psychiatrist's office went through (albeit unsuccessfully), several operations were halted in mid-planning due to their high risk nature. On June 7, 1972, Nixon ordered the burglary of the Brookings Institute, a Washington think-tank, and in the order was his clearly expressed sentiment: "I want the Brookings safe cleared out." He further recommended that Haldeman speak with E. Howard Hunt, described by Haldeman as "ruthless, quiet, careful - kind of a tiger. He spent 20 years in the CIA overthrowing governments." [54] The intended burglary of the Brookings Institute was neither the first nor the gentlest plan to be drawn up; Charles Colson, considered the "evil genius" of the White House staff, initially recommended that the Brookings be firebombed. Ultimately, no attempt was never made.

Meanwhile, the intent to break-into the editor's office of the *Las Vegas Sun* was based on its relationship with billionaire Howard Hughes, whose associate, Robert Meheu, possessed damaging evidence against Democratic presidential candidate Edmund Muskie. This "mission" was halted as well; a general point of strategy, introduced by Gordon Liddy, was voted down by the White House Staff, with John Dean observing that such things should not be discussed within the Office of the Attorney General. The subject matter even included the formation of a prostitution ring in Washington to be used for intelligence gathering.

[53] David von Drehle, Washington Post Politics
[54] History Commons, Watergate - *The White House Plumbers*

Liddy in 1964

John Dean in 1972

On July 7, 1972, E. Howard Hunt was appointed to the White House staff, an appointment that represented a ratcheting up of the hardball style. At the time of Hunt's appointment, Nixon is quoted as saying, "Whoever opposes us, we will destroy. As a matter of fact, anyone who doesn't support us, we will destroy."

Ultimately, Ellsberg would be tried under the Espionage Act of 1917 for the disclosures, but fittingly, the case led to revelations of illegal wiretapping and the attempted burglary of his psychiatrist's office that compelled the judge to dismiss the case against Ellsberg in early May 1973: "The totality of the circumstances of this case which I have only briefly sketched offend a sense of justice. The bizarre events have incurably infected the prosecution of this case." Less than two weeks earlier, those same revelations would force the resignations of Ehrlichman, Haldeman, Dean, and U.S. Attorney General Richard Kleindienst on April 30. Looking back at it all, Ellsberg would later proclaim, "The public is lied to every day by the President, by his spokespeople, by his officers. If you can't handle the thought that the President lies to the public for all kinds of reasons, you couldn't stay in the government at that level, or you're made aware of it, a week. ... The fact is Presidents rarely say the whole truth—essentially, never say the whole truth—of what they expect and what they're doing and what they believe and why they're doing it and rarely refrain from lying, actually, about these matters."

Chapter 8: The Watergate Break-Ins

The Watergate complex

While the attempted burglaries related to Ellsberg would go unnoticed for several months, the break-ins related to the Watergate complex would not. Hunt would later testify that the initial decision to break-into Watergate was because Liddy had received information that "the Cuban government was supplying funds to the Democratic Party", and to "investigate this report, a surreptitious entry of Democratic national headquarters at the Watergate was made."

Although records recently unsealed seem to support Hunt's testimony, Liddy contradicted it, claiming he had received an order from Nixon aide Jeb Magruder to break-in because the Administration "wanted to hear anything that was going on inside the office of Larry O'Brien, who was the chairman of the DNC". Magruder further told Liddy he "wanted to be able to monitor his telephone conversations."

Magruder

As it turned out, Liddy had already considered breaking into Watergate, in an effort to target "the DNC headquarters for later, when and if it became the headquarters of the successful Democratic candidate at their convention". Liddy also recalled telling Magruder he could successfully break-in: "Yes. It's a high-security building, but we can do it." However, due to lack of surviving evidence, it's unclear exactly when Nixon Administration officials first discussed breaking into Watergate, and it's also unclear how many previous break-ins took place before the most famous one. Hunt later seemed confused about the nature of previous attempts in May 1973 when he testified: "I recall something about that, but it seems to me that was more in the nature of a familiarization tour, that McCord took not more than one or two of the men up there and walked them down to the sixth floor to show them the actual door. Then they simply got back into the elevator. It was simply a familiarizing with the operational problem of the two glass doors that opened into the Democratic National headquarters."

However, James McCord's version of events is crucially different. An electronics specialist, he was recruited specifically for such work in order to bug the phone of Democratic Chairman Larry O'Brien and that of R. Spencer Oliver, the Executive Director of the Association of State Democratic Chairmen. The first break-in attempts in May were successful, and Alfred Baldwin, look-out for the operation, would monitor over 200 calls over the next 20 days. McCord soon realized, however, that one of the bugs wasn't working and had to be replaced. In addition to the need for information that could be gained, news had reached him that the Veterans Against the Vietnam War had opened a desk at the Democratic National Committee. McCord argued "that it was worth going in [again] to see what they could discover about the anti-war activists."

McCord

The break-in at the Watergate Hotel on June 17, 1972 was actually a follow-up mission from a previous break-in several weeks prior to repair dysfunctional spy-taps and to photograph further files. However, on this break-in, the simple existence of a piece of tape over a door lock proved to be the origin of the Administration's fall. The tape was noticed by security guard Frank Willis, in charge of patrolling the luxury apartments and offices of the Watergate, and during his first pass of the evening, Willis removed the tape, assuming it had been placed there by one of the maintenance crews. On his second pass, he saw that the tape had been replaced and realized that something was amiss, so he called the Washington, D.C. police.

That evening, five men were arrested for breaking into the headquarters of the Democratic National Committee: Bernard Barker, Virgilio Gonzalez, Eugenio Martinez, James McCord Jr., and Frank Sturgis. The arrest would have remained a completely non-noteworthy case of break-in had not James McCord been carrying in his notebook the telephone number of E. Howard Hunt, thereby linking the crime to a White House staff member close to the president. Furthermore, $100 bills in possession of the five were traced by sequential serial numbers and were easily traced to a bank account of Barker, then to CREEP. Working under the Committee to Re-elect the President (later called CREEP), a fund-raising organization, those arrested represented a membership that included (a) Kenneth Dahlberg, Midwest Finance Chairman, (b) E. Howard Hunt, former agent for the CIA, and now only designated as a "campaign member," (c) Fred LaRue, Campaign Political Operative, (d) G. Gordon Liddy (campaign member) (e) Jeb Stuart Magruder, Campaign Manager, (f) James W. McCord, Campaign Security Coordinator (g) John Mitchell, Campaign Director, (h) Donald Segretti, Campaign Political Operative and (i) Hugh Sloan, Campaign Treasurer. It was Segretti who was predominantly in charge of the various break-ins ordered by CREEP, including an FBI investigation of CBS reporter Daniel Schorr, while Gordon Liddy was behind a largely unformulated plan to assassinate columnist Jack Anderson.

Shortly after the capture, a listening post was discovered at the Howard Johnson across the street from the Watergate, and the look-out man, Alfred Baldwin, was found first. Apparently, Liddy and Hunt were stationed there to remain in communication throughout the operation, and given that several of the conspirators were former agents in the CIA, suspicion immediately grew about just how "former" they really were. Barker's codename was AMCLATTER-1 in CIA files, and he had been a paid agent since 1966. Gonzalez was a former agent, and Martinez was a current agent. Hunt, the most high-level agent of all, could not be officially pinned down, listed in CREEP as only a "member." In all, over half a million dollars would be spent by CREEP in lawyer fees alone in the trials of these five, and the linking of lawyer fees to the administration provided the second spark that moved the Watergate story forward.

Chapter 9: The Administration's Initial Coverup Attempts

"A third rate burglary attempt." – Ron Ziegler, White House Press Secretary

Bob Woodward was present at the five arraignments "and overheard McCord mention CIA in connection with his occupation."[55] It was this revelation that compelled him to continue investigating, and as he was beginning his initial work, the coverup of the burglary attempt was

---

[55] U.S. History.com - Watergate Scandal - www.u-s-history.com/page/h1791.html

already underway. It seems Nixon was unaware of the activities that led to the Watergate break-in, and in a meeting on June 23, Nixon asked Haldeman, "Who was the asshole who ordered it?" However, the inclusion of Hunt's name forced the Administration to scramble immediately after the arrests took place. Dean claimed Ehrlichman ordered him to destroy records related to Hunt, and though Ehrlichman denied that, the evidence was ultimately destroyed by the White House Counsel and the FBI's Acting Director, L. Patrick Gray. "Magruder and others destroyed documents and lied to investigators."[56] Nixon also instructed Haldeman to obstruct the FBI investigation when he realized that John Mitchell, head of CREEP, was involved. Mitchell immediately resigned for "personal reasons."

In McCord's view, the president took matters in a fateful direction following the arrests by attempting to disguise the break-in as a CIA operation, which could not possibly hold up without the CIA falsely backing up his story. While Nixon might have believed that possible, McCord believed the right people were not in place for that to occur, and sensing what was about to happen, McCord wrote a hurried letter to Jack Caulfield, the Assistant Director of Crime Enforcement, telling him that if "[CIA Director Richard] Helms goes, and if the operation is laid at the CIA's feet, where it does not belong, every tree in the forest will fall. It will be a scorched desert." Nevertheless, Nixon went to Helms in an attempt to force the CIA to pay hush money for the five arrestees at the Watergate, and while others at the agency were willing to go along with that, Helms flatly refused. Helms later pointed out that the CIA " could get the money. ... We didn't need to launder money...[but] the end result would have been the end of the agency. Not only would I have gone to jail if I had gone along with what the White House wanted us to do, but the agency's credibility would have been ruined forever." In typical Nixonian fashion, efforts to remove Helms from the CIA started immediately, and eventually he lost his job as Director of Central Intelligence in February 1973. As McCord predicted, every tree in the forest would fall with him.

---

[56] U.S. History.com - Watergate Scandal

Helms

Nixon also had to worry about the 1972 presidential election against George McGovern that November. On August 29, Nixon announced that his White House Counsel, John Dean, had investigated the break-in and claimed, "I can say categorically that... no one in the White House staff, no one in this Administration, presently employed, was involved in this very bizarre incident." Nixon further praised Dean on September 15, "The way you've handled it, it seems to me, has been very skillful, because you—putting your fingers in the dikes every time that leaks have sprung here and sprung there." In fact, far from conducting any semblance of an investigation, Dean was actively working to obstruct one by destroying evidence.

Ultimately, the initial coverup efforts were successful through the election. Although more information kept coming out tying the Watergate burglary attempt to men affiliated with CREEP, and financial records also showed the way in which money was being moved, Nixon's reelection campaign was never in jeopardy. Even as indictments were handed down to the five conspirators, Nixon won in a landslide over McGovern, and despite the fact Liddy and McCord were about to be convicted for a wide range of crimes, including burglary and illegal wire-tapping, the coverup successfully contained the full breadth of the White House's work behind the scenes. Of course, if anything, Nixon's historic landslide showed just how needless his Administration's attempts to go after its political enemies were.

Nixon had been reelected, but his problems with Watergate were just beginning.

Chapter 10: Nixon's Second Term and the Unraveling of the Watergate Coverup

Despite a severe recession, energy concerns and a serious rate of inflation, Nixon was easily re-elected to a second term in 1972 after a series of wage and price freezes. Theoretically, at least, Nixon's second term should have been a powerhouse; despite a confrontational Congress, he "returned to the White House...constitutionally his last four year term of office as an unusually strong president, one of the strongest the United States has ever had."[57] For such a vision of the second term, the landscape was ideal. The seemingly endless Vietnam conflict was over at last, for which Nixon received much credit. Re-election was no longer a concern, and the president enjoyed historically high numbers in tandem with a robust economy and low unemployment.

One statistic that suggested a constant distrust of Nixon was reflected in the voter turnout percentage of 55%, but he seemed unperturbed by either this or the high degree of Congressional rancor. Having achieved reelection, in which he captured large liberal factions as well, Nixon was now free to shed his former liberal rhetoric and trend toward the conservative views where he was more comfortable. Only two months after his election victory, he was barely recognizable as the more familiar moderate model, and believing he no longer needed public or governmental support, "Mr. Nixon withdrew into himself even more than usual - he was always an aloof president."[58] He seemed to view the press with equal indifference during this period, and major actions, such as the bombing of North Vietnam, had already gone by with no press conferences. Never a friend of the press, he finally felt able drop them from his list of burdens and even to exact some revenge through neglect.

In 1974, the budget presented by the president "curtailed about a hundred existing programmes."[59] Nixon cut off agricultural subsidies, "slum clearance, job training, education for the disadvantaged, health care for the old - which made up President Johnson's package of Great Society legislation."[60] A new plan to reshuffle government into four divisions with no shared responsibilities collided with the status quo involving a large number of entrenched bureaucrats, and he dismissed a number of first term Cabinet members, such as George Romney and John Volpe, who had disagreed with the president in earlier conflicts and were considered to be too independent. During this time, the nickname "King Richard" came to be a common description heard in Washington..

As a way of meeting majority opposition in the legislative branch, Nixon honed the art of

---

[57] Nancy Balfour, "President Nixon's Second Term", in *The World Today*, Vol. 29 no. 3, March'73, p. 98
[58] The World Today, p. 98
[59] The World Today, p. 100
[60] The World Today p. 100

"executive privilege" and moved forward on many fronts, employing it as an end run around all opposition. Even power over the purse, nominally exercised by the House, was not a deterrent because the president's agenda involved a great deal more cutting than spending. "This matter of executive privilege [was] a traditional source of friction, but [was] bound to be intensified, now that so much of the business of government [was] to be conducted in the presidential offices."[61]

Nixon further attempted to reduce nominating powers of the Senate, which in turn demanded restoration and increased nominee testimony at hearings. In this, the natural parallel to executive privilege, the question of executive transparency grew as a serious concern. However, when the first whiff of the Watergate controversy emerged in connection to the White House - an administration that had been re-elected by 520 electoral votes, had overseen the Paris Peace Accord and two summits with Soviet premier Leonid Brezhnev, had conducted a fruitful search for a general peace in the Middle East, and had even realized John F. Kennedy's dream of putting a man on the moon - fell into an increasingly rapid death spiral.

The Nixon Administration's immediate attempts to coverup the extent of its involvement would not begin to unravel for well over another year. Even though Woodward and Carl Bernstein reported on the scandal throughout the summer and continued to receive information from Deep Throat, connections to the president gained little traction. The *Washington Post* was still isolated in the battle with the White House, and no other major newspapers seemed interested, but despite the advantage of having a direct line to Felt, the two famous reporters have claimed in retrospect that what was received from Deep Throat served mostly to confirm information from other sources. Although Nixon would later claim "Watergate would have been a blip" if he was a Democrat, media interest in the story was initially low; even though Felt also leaked details to other publications like *Time*, most outlets wouldn't really start running with Watergate until they caught wind that one of the men implicated had alleged they were part of a high-profile conspiracy and coverup.

---

[61] The World Today, p. 104

Woodward

Gradually, as suspicion grew that the Watergate break-in was a more far-reaching conspiracy, the Senate voted to conduct an investigation following Acting FBI Director Gray's testimony before they confirmed him for the permanent position of FBI Director. His testimony implicated several of the White House staff, and on March 21, 1973, John Dean wrote to the president describing the escalating controversy as "a cancer growing on the presidency." Meanwhile, as the five men arrested for the break-in found themselves being positioned to take the fall, not to mention lengthy prison sentences, they started to make waves as well. Hunt began to make rumblings of confessions that could only be forestalled by hush money, after which he almost immediately received $75,000. Hunt's wife Dorothy was deeply involved as well; on the morning of December 8, 1972, she and her daughter Teresa were killed in a plane crash while carrying $10,000 in $100 bills, all meant to be used as hush money. Hunt and others insisted that it was money for a real estate investment, but before boarding the plane, she purchased a life insurance policy that paid $250,000 upon her death and made her husband beneficiary. Her strange death is a never-ending source of fascination for conspiracy theorists who suspect that she was murdered by the Administration; one such report claims that "moments after impact, a battalion of plainclothes operatives in unmarked cars parked on side streets pounced on the crash site." McCord would later claim in his book, *A Piece of Tape - the Watergate Story: Fact and*

Fiction, that Dorothy Hunt possessed information about the president of such magnitude that it would almost certainly result in his impeachment. It is also surprising that in this book, which McCord wasted no time in writing (having it published in 1974), "Former CIA officer Miles Copland claimed that had he [McCord] had led the Watergate burglars into a trap, and that Helms had prior knowledge of the break-in."

The trial began on January 8, 1973 and sported a colorful cast of characters, beginning with Judge John Sirica, a former boxer who was well-known for doling out strict sentences. He had worked in the U.S. Attorney's office during the Hoover administration despite losing his first 13 cases as a court-appointed attorney, and known as a maverick Republican, many of his decisions were later overturned. Considered unpredictable by the legal world, the term "Maximum John" followed him through his career. During the trial, Sirica created an enduring conflict when he met secretly with the Watergate Committee prosecutor, Leon Jaworski, and the judge stirred the pot even more when he took to questioning witnesses himself after finding their testimony uninformative and of dubious integrity.

Meanwhile, in an effort to get ahead of the scandal, the president made a March 1 announcement that he was initiating his own investigation of Watergate, but the day after, he instructed U.S. Attorney General John Mitchell, "I want you to stonewall it; let them plead the Fifth Amendment; cover-up or anything else, if it'll save it; save the plan." By this time, federal agents had already discovered the Nixon administration slush fund to sponsor attacks on various foes of the White House, and the money trail was traced to the top line in the Attorney General's Office: John Mitchell himself. Mitchell was an old law partner of Nixon, and he had also been the commander of John F. Kennedy's PT Boat unit. Before the Watergate affair, he had worked with issues of segregation and affirmative action, but Mitchell would be indicted in May 1973 and convicted of conspiracy to obstruct justice, perjury, and obstruction of justice, ultimately serving 19 months in prison. Before his conviction, Mitchell had tried to get the *Washington Post* to spike a story about the slush fund, warning that Katharine Graham, the *Washington Post*'s publisher, would have a sensitive area of her body "caught in a big fat wringer if that's published."

Mitchell about to testify before the Senate Watergate Committee in 1963

About a month after the beginning of the Watergate trial, on February 7, the Senate voted 77 - 0 to create a Select Committee on Presidential Campaign Activities. The Committee was to be headed by Sam Ervin of North Carolina, who would become a national TV icon thanks to the daily broadcasts from the capital. Although the public perceived of him as a relaxed grandfatherly type, Ervin was a hard-nosed, decorated soldier from World War I and a Harvard Law graduate. Of particular offense to Ervin was Nixon's continued refusal to testify before the committee or to allow his staff to testify, citing executive privilege, national security and any other legal mechanism he could think up. Referring to the Nixon subordinates' refusal to offer information, Ervin was particularly incensed: "Divine right of kings went out with the American Revolution and doesn't belong to White House aides - that is not executive privilege, that is executive poppycock!"

Ervin

It may have been that the hierarchical Nixon felt that he could more successfully exert pressure upon the Watergate prosecutors than on the chairman of the committee, as Ervin seemed impervious to political, social or media press. He was thought by many in the Senate to be the perfect candidate for the job, having gathered enormous respect from both sides of the aisle over his many years of service. His description of the Committee's mandate early on left no doubt as to his intent: "My colleagues on the Committee are determined to uncover all the relevant facts surrounding these matters, and to spare no one, whatever his position in life may be." In subsequent writings about Watergate, which include *The Whole Truth: The Watergate Conspiracy*, *Humor of a Country Lawyer*, and *Preserving the Constitution*, Ervin expressed one major regret regarding the outcome of the proceedings: "Congress did not do more to restrict the president's executive privilege."

The president would seemingly have had a better chance with the Assistant Chairman of the Watergate Committee, Republican Howard Baker of Tennessee, but Baker was able to conduct himself properly throughout, awkward as it might have been for him. Nixon's campaign literature for 1972 hailed Baker as a trusted friend and advisor to the president, but Baker never hindered Ervin's relentless pursuit of the president and his staff. In fact, it was Baker who coined the famous phrase, "What did the President know, and when did he know it?"

As the investigations were beginning, Nixon started to see that more proactive steps were necessary, but another big blow came in the middle of March. The Watergate incident might have died out without reaching the executive level had not John McCord written his personal note to Judge Sirica on March 19, based on the probability that he faced an extensive prison term after initially refusing to cooperate. After the attempt to strong-arm the CIA, which had resulted in the sacking of Richard Helms, McCord was entirely isolated with no protection, so he followed through with his previous threat against the president to abandon the collective secrecy of the action and tell all.

His letter to Judge Sirica was filed in *United States v. George Gordon Libby* in the District Court of Washington, D.C., and opened simply, "to Judge Sirica." In the sudden change to a cooperative tone, McCord cited the conflicting circumstances in which he was trapped, describing himself as "whipsawed in a variety of legalities." Among these, he included the possibility of future testimony being required of him before the Senate Committee, becoming the object of a later civil suit, and of his testimony becoming a matter of record within the Senate via the probation officer, specifically confidential communications between judge and defendant. McCord qualified these sentiments, however, by citing that "on the other hand, to fail to answer your questions may appear to be non-cooperation, and I can therefore expect a much more severe sentence."[62] McCord added alleged fears on the part of his family for his safety and well-being, and although he claimed not to share it, he did express an expectation of certain retaliations against those close to him: "Such retaliations could destroy careers, income, and reputations of persons who are innocent of any guilt whatever."[63]

McCord continued by itemizing certain truths which he felt were not possible to divulge in public testimony due to pressure exerted upon the defendants by those at the federal level. The first item was quoted directly: "There was political pressure applied to defendants to plead guilty and remain silent." The second point was a claim that perjury had been committed by the defendants "in matters highly material to the very structure, orientation and impact of the government's case, and to the motivation and intent of the defendants."[64]

---

[62] Watergate.info - James McCord
[63] Watergate. info - James McCord

McCord's third point was that certain individuals were not identified in courtroom testimony that could have been identified by those testifying. He further claimed that although the Cuban participants might have been led to believe that Watergate was a CIA operation, he knew for a fact that it was not. In another point, McCord described one individual's testimony as a case of "honest errors of memory," although the testifier was perceived as telling untruths. Finally, he explained his previous actions as subject to the circumstances under which his defense was forced to be prepared.

His agenda fully itemized, McCord requested a private meeting in chambers with Sirica following the sentencing phase, and that his speaking with an FBI agent or before a grand jury (and the attending U.S. Attorneys) or other government representatives would be unacceptable. He maintained that no discussion involving such a meeting had taken place with his attorneys, for the sake of their protection, and that he offered his statement "freely and voluntarily."[65] In his time before the committee, McCord offered testimony on many of the accomplished and planned actions underwritten by the White House.

Thus, in his letter to Sirica, McCord had claimed that the defendants were pressured by White House staff to plead guilty and avoid being forthcoming on any salient point of the event. He further charged that the defendants had been forced to perjure themselves for "higher-ups." This letter changed the course of Watergate in two ways. First, the event brought the break-in outside of the Washington beltway and fueled the larger public imagination, and second, it changed the face of Watergate from a criminal investigation to a political bombshell. The *Washington Post* would never again find itself alone in its interest.

In mid-April, Jeb Magruder was feeling the heat, and in turn he implicated John Dean and Attorney General John Mitchell. In turn, just a few days later, John Dean informed Nixon that he too was now cooperating with authorities, and that same day, authorities informed the Administration that Haldeman, Ehrlichman, Dean and others had all been implicated as part of a high-level coverup. Naturally, in an effort to distance himself from them, Nixon asked these White House officials to resign. By separating from them, he hoped he could turn any subsequent investigations into his own actions as being his word against theirs.

One of the items that unnerved John Dean the most was McCord's letter to Judge Sirica, and he began to warn Nixon repeatedly that things were getting out of control, as "his resolve wilted." Shortly after, Dean agreed to cooperate with prosecutors on April 6 under an agreement of limited immunity. Within his testimony of the following month would be a claim that he had discussed the workings of a cover-up with the President himself. In fact, he estimated that he had discussed it with Nixon approximately 35 times.

[64] Watergate.info
[65] Watergate.info

The straightforwardness of Dean's testimony could be ascribed to a number of motivations, from a sense of conscience to the strategy of being coolly truthful and not overplaying the nobility of breaking open the corruption. When Senator Talmedge commented to Dean in session that "in finding evidence of a conspirator of this magnitude, it was incumbent upon you as a counsel to the president that he got that information at the time," Dean simply responded, "Senator, I was participating in a cover-up at that time."[66] When asked in the same session whether Dean felt that his conscience was clear, his answer combined ethics and self-survival, claiming that he "could not endure perjury upon perjury upon perjury...I wasn't capable of doing that, and I knew that my day of being called was not far off."[67]

In addition to his conversations with the president, Dean suggested a similar body of conversations with Patrick Gray, Assistant Director of the FBI, on the same subject. Gray had admitted such in the hearings for his appointment to Director of the FBI, and his nomination was ultimately rejected. Dean's first day testimony of seven hours not only clearly implicated the president in the cover-up but was the first bald assertion that the subject of the cover-up could be found in presidential conversations on the White House tapes.

A few months into 1973, Nixon was confident that he was almost done with Watergate and would soon never have to speak of it again, but he now realized he had to take more proactive steps. On April 17, the president announced that in a change of heart, his staff would appear before the Watergate Committee, although the same reticence to testify would hold true. The same day, Nixon claimed that he had no prior knowledge of the incident on any level. And on April 30, Nixon announced the resignations of Dean, Haldeman, and Ehrlichman, stating, "In one of the most difficult decisions of my Presidency, I accepted the resignations of two of my closest associates in the White House, Bob Haldeman, John Ehrlichman, two of the finest public servants it has been my privilege to know. Because Attorney General Kleindienst, though a distinguished public servant, my personal friend for 20 years, with no personal involvement whatsoever in this matter has been a close personal and professional associate of some of those who are involved in this case, he and I both felt that it was also necessary to name a new Attorney General. The Counsel to the President, John Dean, has also resigned." After the speech, Nixon was quoted as consoling Haldeman, "Well, it's a tough thing, Bob, for you, for John, and the rest...but goddamnit, I'm never going to discuss this son-of-a-bitch Watergate thing again...never, never, never, never."

Chapter 11: Catching Up With Nixon

As the links widened and pointed toward consistent executive involvement, containment

---

[66] NBClearn
[67] NBClearn[67]
[67] NBClearn

became exponentially more difficult, and it seemed as though every new instance of the White House digging in its heels was met with a new revelation causing circumstances to slip out of its control. On June 13, a memo was discovered in which Ehrlichman's plans to break-into the office of Daniel Ellsberg's psychiatrist was discovered, and John Dean's seven-hour statement to the committee had already turned Nixon into the committee's principal target, not to mention his own testimony. As late as July 7, Nixon still refused to appear before the panel, and rejected all demands for presidential documents.

This latest stalemate, however, was broken wide open by the discovery of the president's secret taping system in the White House, one previously employed by John F. Kennedy. The taping system had been implemented to archive the thoughts of all those in White House meetings, but now it was clearly a key piece of evidence that would clearly show the president's depth of involvement. The knowledge of a taping system was somewhat innocently explained to the committee by former White House Appointments Secretary Alexander Butterfield, and it was quickly discovered that the tapes of White House meetings and calls went back to 1971.

By now, the sentiment that the Watergate break-in was not nearly as serious as the White House coverup became a rallying cry for large anti-White House segments of the population, and for the committee. Those intent on tracing the crime to the top of the executive branch smelled blood. On August 15, Nixon was before the cameras again, this time extolling before the public the importance of confidentiality in executive dealings, but over the next several weeks, the two years of taped presidential conversations occupied the center of the investigations. Even as they became the object of a subpoena, Nixon disconnected the system on July 26, a week before the subpoena for the tapes.

Not surprisingly, Nixon's August appearance made little difference to the judiciary, and Judge Sirica demanded that the White House turn over the entire collection on August 29. The committee continued to insist that he turn them over as well, having won every legal step toward taking possession of them thus far.

As the legal arguments over that subpoena were ongoing, Nixon lost his strongest attack dog on October 10 with the resignation of Vice President Spiro Agnew, who resigned his office after pleading no contest to charges of income tax evasion. A Marylander, Agnew was a popular choice for the ticket in the South. At first glance, his inclusion as an attack dog against various opposition groups fit Nixon's combative style perfectly, but he also bypassed the opportunity for gaining favor and winning friends, something at which Nixon was extraordinarily clumsy. Before allegations of fraudulent financial practices hit Agnew, he symbolized the righteousness of the administration, lashing out at the anti-war movement, but unfortunately, he did not stop at what was considered a nation-wide adolescent rebellion. So pervasive were his tirades, written for the most part by speechwriters Pat Buchanan and William Safire, that he took on the persona of "a tough-talking, intensely negative public presence in Washington." [68] His descriptions of collegiate protesters as "an effete corps of impudent snobs who characterize themselves as intellectuals...[who] take their tactics from Fidel Castro and their money from daddy" resonated with middle-aged and older Americans. Attacking the national press, however, was damaging to a faction much needed by the Administration.

Still, Agnew's alliterative descriptions of the "nattering nabobs of negativism" caught the public fascination, even though he was disliked. One Baltimore patron, asked whether he hoped Agnew would become president, responded that he didn't want a president who sounded like he did after a few beers. Railing against general enemies of the White House, Agnew employed phrases such as "pusillanimous pussy-footers," "vicars of vacillation" and ideological eunuchs." Even these lines were crossed, however, as the Baltimore street-talking style entered the arena of racial slurs against several groups, including Asians and Poles.

In time, even Nixon himself realized that Agnew, a regular complainer about the disrespect he felt in the White House, was a liability, and so he pressured Agnew to resign. Agnew resisted at first, and he even blamed White House staff for conspiring against him. Nixon attempted to replace him with Texas Governor John Connally, a victim (and hero) of the Kennedy assassination, but Connally wasn't interested in the office, calling it "useless." Agnew eventually agreed to resign if provided with guarantees against being prosecuted.

Thus, with Agnew out, on October 12th, Gerald Ford was nominated to replace Agnew, the very same day the U.S. Circuit Court of Appeals ruled that the entire body of tapes must be turned over. The man who had subpoenaed the tapes was Special Prosecutor Archibald Cox, who had been the eighth person sought out by Attorney General Elliott Richardson for the position of Special Prosecutor. Cox was Richardson's old law professor, and Cox's great-grandfather, William Maxwell Evarts, had defended Andrew Johnson in his impeachment, barely saving him from conviction. In Cox, Nixon would find yet another obstacle that he could not move via political or legal bullying, and he also harbored a particular mistrust of Cox due to his ties to the Kennedys, as the Prosecutor had served as an advisor for Congressman John F. Kennedy over a decade earlier. Cox had no intention of budging on the White House's compromise of edited tapes, particularly since the editing was to be done by one of Nixon's people, and on top of that, the president further stipulated that Cox would call for no further evidence.

Cox

Nixon viewed Cox as an increasing menace and attempted to remove him, thinking that the head of the committee being absent might lessen the pressure. This led to a series of severe White House actions in the month of October, culminating in what came to be known as the Saturday Night Massacre. Nixon desperately sought some high-ranking official in the judicial system who would forcibly remove Archibald Cox from the Senate Committee. The president personally called Attorney General Elliott Richardson and instructed him to make the firing happen. When the Attorney General refused, he was fired over the phone. Following that, the president called the Assistant Attorney General, William Ruckelshaus, who also refused and was fired. At last, someone was found who would do the deed: Acting Attorney General Robert Bork. Bork removed Cox from the committee. Clearly, Bork had learned from the previous two men being fired that his ability to stay in office required following the president's order, though he later claimed he considered resigning to avoid being "perceived as a man who did the President's bidding to save my job." Regardless, he appointed Leon Jaworski to take Cox's place.

The "Massacre" received widespread public criticism, and the first serious calls for the president's impeachment were now beginning heard. The following week, an irate Congress called for impeachment as well, introducing 22 resolutions to that effect. Cox was elevated to the level of an American hero, "the last honest man in Washington". Again, the president had exercised his skill in retaliation, but he had utterly neglected to garner support, either inside or outside of the Beltway. Cox's official response to his removal was terse; invoking John Adams, he said, "Whether ours shall continue to be a government of laws and not men is now before

Congress and ultimately before the American people."[69]

On October 23, with the walls closing in on him, Nixon appeared to relent by releasing a portion of the tapes, but it was quickly apparent that none of these tapes had any significant pertinence to the matter at hand. At this point, a series of suspicious irregularities occurred, such as claims that specific tapes on the list did not exist. The famous 18 minute gap, when investigated, met with conflicting answers from secretary Rosemary Woods and other White House officials. Chief of Staff Alexander Haig "credited the gap to 'some sinister force,'"[70] which he did not specify. Regardless, the announcement of an 18 minute gap, suggesting five separate erasures, was announced by the White House on November 21. Woods, the curator of the tapes, denied any involvement in the missing archives.

Ultimately, firing Cox led Nixon nowhere. When Jaworski took over for Archibald Cox on November 1, via an appointment made by Robert Bork (former Solicitor General and third in line behind the Attorney General), he proved to be every bit as insistent as his predecessor, and he immediately called for full disclosure of the tapes.

Jaworski

In the month of November, the tug-of-war continued between the judicial and executive branches, and following the Christmas break, the House of Representatives instructed the Judiciary Committee to investigate the viability of impeachment against the president, congruent

---

[69] The Washington Post; *Archibald Cox* - www.washingtonpost.com
[70] Gerald R. Ford Library and Museum

with all the other investigations then taking place with the court case, Jaworski and the committee. By the beginning of March, seven White House aides had been indicted on 13 counts of obstructing an investigation. Nixon being named by Jaworski as an "un-indicted co-conspirator" did not place the president in immediate jeopardy, but it was lethal in terms of public opinion.

The president released the previously offered transcripts, heavily edited, and followed their emergence with another television appearance, much like the last one. However, with the materials that had come out, however, Nixon's likeability among the larger population was taking an enormous hit, due in no small part to the unexpected vulgarity of his language on the recordings. From this collective realization came the now famous phrase "expletive deleted." An editorial in the *Chicago Tribune* complained, "He is humorless to the point of being inhumane. He is devious. He is vacillating. He is profane. He is willing to be led. He displays dismaying gaps in knowledge. He is suspicious of his staff. His loyalty is minimal."

Nixon knew, without a doubt, that the process of impeachment, initiated by the House and tried by the Senate, not only depended on high crimes and misdemeanors but the detailed documentation of such. The physical possession of the tapes was essential to that distinction, for without such a level of evidence, "the linkage between presidential misdemeanors performed by the president is neither automatic nor obvious."[71] Even at this late date, he believed he was able to control them. What he was no longer able to manipulate, however, despite a history of brilliant game-saving television appearances, was public opinion and various factions of institutional support. He certainly was aware that "other things being equal, popular presidents are more capable of enduring accusations," With the tapes given up and with the new public perception of his personal style, Nixon had spent or wasted his remaining political capital.

Impeachment hearings began in early March of 1974 in the Judiciary, assisted by material provided by Sirica's court. Jaworski, meanwhile, "appealed to the Supreme Court to force Nixon to surrender more tapes."[72] A decision was not received until July 24, but by a vote of 8 - 0, the court upheld the request for the turnover of the tapes. Quickly after that, three articles of impeachment came down from the House: "Obstructing the Watergate investigation; misuse of power and violating the oath of office; failure to comply with House subpoenas."[73]

Finally, on the 5th of August, Nixon released the remaining tapes, but only after considering far more rash last-minute actions against the Supreme Court. All in all, the White House tapes cover a period of "2 years - 3700 hours of phone calls and meetings. 2,371 are declassified."[74] Highlighted conversations, now available on many internet sources, include brashly profane and

---

[71] Victor J. Hinohosa, Anibal S. Perez-Linan, "Presidential Survival and the Impeachment Process", in *Political Science Quarterly* Vol. 121, no. 4 Winter 2006, p.655

[72] Gerald R. Ford Library and Museum

[73] Gerald R. Ford Library and Museum

[74] Nixontapes.org

vulgar attempts on the president's part to both understand what is happening to him and to control it through the force of his office. The most important tapes, now available for listen all over the internet, include the "smoking gun" conversation of June 23, 1972, a conversation about tracing money back to the White House from those bills found in the burglars' possession. Other important recordings include the January 1973 excerpt in which Charles Colson explains why George McGovern had to be bugged, the March 21 "Cancer on the presidency" warnings of John Dean, including discussion of hush money payments to Hunt and others. In that one, Nixon suggests the blackmail money should be paid: "…just looking at the immediate problem, don't you have to have – handle Hunt's financial situation damn soon? […] you've got to keep the cap on the bottle that much, in order to have any options." There is also the March 27 discussion of John Mitchell's involvement, and an April 16 discussion on how to stall the investigation and deal with the Dean problem. More tapes continue to be declassified, including as recently as 340 hours in 2013.

Of the released tapes, one of the first to receive recognition was recorded only a few days after the break-in: the "smoking gun" conversation with H.R. Haldeman that was damning enough for Nixon's remaining support in the Senate to crumble. In it, Haldeman can be heard telling Nixon, "the Democratic break-in thing, we're back to the–in the, the problem area because the FBI is not under control, because Gray doesn't exactly know how to control them, and they have… their investigation is now leading into some productive areas […] and it goes in some directions we don't want it to go." With that, as Fred Buzhardt and James St. Clair put it, "The tape proved that the President had lied to the nation, to his closest aides, and to his own lawyers – for more than two years."

On the night of August 7, several Congressmen, including Senators Barry Goldwater and Hugh Scott, met with Nixon to tell him that he would certainly be impeached in the House and convicted in the Senate. Thus, the next day, the president announced his resignation from office:

> "In all the decisions I have made in my public life, I have always tried to do what was best for the Nation. Throughout the long and difficult period of Watergate, I have felt it was my duty to persevere, to make every possible effort to complete the term of office to which you elected me. In the past few days, however, it has become evident to me that I no longer have a strong enough political base in the Congress to justify continuing that effort. As long as there was such a base, I felt strongly that it was necessary to see the constitutional process through to its conclusion, that to do otherwise would be unfaithful to the spirit of that deliberately difficult process and a dangerously destabilizing precedent for the future….

> I would have preferred to carry through to the finish whatever the personal agony it would have involved, and my family unanimously urged me to do so. But the interest of the Nation must always come before any personal considerations. From

the discussions I have had with Congressional and other leaders, I have concluded that because of the Watergate matter I might not have the support of the Congress that I would consider necessary to back the very difficult decisions and carry out the duties of this office in the way the interests of the Nation would require.

I have never been a quitter. To leave office before my term is completed is abhorrent to every instinct in my body. But as President, I must put the interest of America first. America needs a full-time President and a full-time Congress, particularly at this time with problems we face at home and abroad. To continue to fight through the months ahead for my personal vindication would almost totally absorb the time and attention of both the President and the Congress in a period when our entire focus should be on the great issues of peace abroad and prosperity without inflation at home. Therefore, I shall resign the Presidency effective at noon tomorrow. Vice President Ford will be sworn in as President at that hour in this office."

As a result of Watergate, 69 government officials would be indicted, and 48 would be convicted of some crime. Among all the White House conspirators, Richard Nixon remained free of further court actions, thanks to a full pardon the following year from then President Gerald R. Ford. Ford justified that controversial decision by calling Nixon's plight and potential ongoing criminal investigation "an American tragedy in which we all have played a part. It could go on and on and on, or someone must write the end to it. I have concluded that only I can do that, and if I can, I must."

A 1976 campaign button referencing Ford's pardon of Nixon

Chapter 12: The Impact of Watergate

Calmer voices, such as that of the steady-minded Adlai Stevenson, refer to the Watergate era as one "in which we reacted not to history, but to aberrations of history." The decade is viewed as one in which great institutional shifts took place, and one in which executive powers were wrested from the presidency in general. In retrospect, much is said of the networking of the White House staff; where they were once designed to sustain efficiency, the 1970s increasingly turned them into an institutional mover of policy, political gamesmanship, camouflage and deflection. George Reedy, two years before the Watergate break-in, warned that "one of Mr. Nixon's biggest mistakes was in enlarging the White House Staff."[75]

Author Walter Lippman suggested that corruption in national governments represents a fairly steady topography, but that " a community governs itself by fits and starts of unsuspecting complacency and violent suspicion." All this is to say that the Nixon administration thrived during a period of the latter, and Victor Lasky agreed with that view in "It Didn't Start with Watergate" (1977), suggesting that Richard Nixon was in no way unusual and that all the events occurring in that era had occurred regularly before. Pro-Nixon conservatives, who observed the rise in reporter freedom among the nation's major newspapers and the media's ability to diminish the integrity of public figures through rabid journalism by rooting out "public

---

[75] Gordon Hoxie, *Presidential Studies Quarterly*

misconduct," claim that the habit had its origins during the Taft and Theodore Roosevelt administrations, impelled by "professional writers who portrayed themselves as objective servers of society, reporting conditions as they found them."

Former Nixon official Geoff Shepard, in his book *The Secret Plot to Make Ted Kennedy President*, claimed that Watergate as a whole was much more about Democratic political maneuvering than it was about White House crimes, and that Sirica's improprieties were blatant, as he met with the Watergate Special Prosecutor in a behind-the-scenes farce of "secret meetings, secret documents, [and] secret collusion."[76] He suggests overall that no fair trials were ever received or intended, and that the real intent of the proceedings was to gain a stronger hold on Congress and injure the Republican party beyond repair. The book, in fact, is dedicated "to the thousands of Republicans...whose aspirations were thwarted, whose careers were ended, and whose lives were ruined in the single-minded effort to destroy them and the GOP - to the end that Ted Kennedy might become president, and the restoration of Camelot finally be achieved."[77]

Whichever side of the press debate one is on, it is undeniable that national press, in particular the *Washington Post*, brought the otherwise small incident of an office burglary to light, and it is commonly thought that if the *Post* had not served as David to the White House's Goliath, the whole thing might very well have blown over. The question of why the incident did not die a quick and mostly overlooked death endures; by September 1972, only 52% of the public had even heard of the Watergate break-in, but by June of 1973, almost all Americans were intimately aware of both the incident and of the ongoing judicial process. George McGovern made corruption a theme in his presidential campaign in 1972, but even then, he did not specifically address Watergate, and by 1974, the energy crisis in America could very easily have served as the replacement story to an already aging Watergate saga.

In some quarters, among liberals and journalists, the press is hailed as an enormous moving force, and in most cases, a heroic one. Conversely, others believe to this day that the press did not play more than a modest role in ending the Nixon administration. Regardless, there was an additional reason for the *Washington Post* holding the inside track on the Watergate investigation. Not only did they function centrally within the Beltway, but they had an unimaginably fortuitous source within the top levels of government, one of which no other journalistic institution could boast. Martin Kalb, of Harvard's Shorenstein Center of the Press, Politics and Public Policy, believed that the *Washington Post*'s general push to air deeper aspects of the scandal was "absolutely critical to creating an atmosphere in Washington and within the government that Nixon was in serious trouble, and that the White House was engaged in a cover-up."[78] Indeed, it was the refusal to back down or let go of the subject that Woodward and Bernstein, representing the Post in the face of numerous federal threats, kept the pursuit of the

[76] Geoff Shephard, "The Secret Plot to Make Ted Kennedy President: Inside the *Real* Watergate Conspiracy, Penguin Group: New York, 2008

[77] Geoff Shepard, "The Secret Plot to Make Ted Kennedy President: The *Real* Watergate Conspiracy"

[78] Mark Feldstein, *Watergate Revisited,* aijarchive.com, 2004-www.aijarchive.org/article.asp?id=3735

scandal's hidden layers moving forward. According to one pro-journalist source, Woodward and Bernstein "produced the single most spectacular act of serious journalism [in the 20th century]."[79] And of course, Woodward and Bernstein eventually published the defining book of the era on the subject, *All the President's Men*, which was sensationalized in a film with Robert Redmond and Dustin Hoffman and captured the public's fascination with "Deep Throat," a clearly well-informed source whose identity would remain secret for nearly 30 years after the events in question.

As the Watergate era fades into history, it is surprising how many of the important players who remain are still active as journalists, biographers and activists. Of course, the central figure in the scandal, Richard Nixon, suffered a stroke in 1994 and died shortly after, but one of his most important victims, Daniel Ellsberg, the leaker of the Pentagon Papers, occupies a nobler place in modern society than he once did (though his status as a traitor or hero for "delegitimizing" the Vietnam War have vehement advocates on both sides of the question). Like many involved in the Watergate era, he continued to work as an activist and was at one point arrested in an Iraq War protest. He consistently lends support to modern "leakers" of government documents, including Edward Snowden, and almost without exception is pro-transparency.

The important White House source who contributed so much primary knowledge to the work of Woodward and Bernstein, Mark Felt, died in 2008 at the age of 95. Felt witnessed the beginnings of modern technology and all the recent events and discoveries of the modern age. Convicted for pursuing alleged members of the Weather Underground without warrants on repeated occasions, he was pardoned by then President Ronald Reagan. Woodward and Bernstein had agreed to keep his identity anonymous, but that became unnecessary when Felt announced himself as Deep Throat in 2005 and continued to release information at the urging of his family.

In terms of mystery and fascination over the scandal, E. Howard Hunt may be the most enigmatic character of the entire era, even more than Deep Throat. Known as the "ultimate keeper of secrets," Hunt died in Miami, January 23, 2007, of pneumonia. Hedegaard alleges that Hunt spent ten years as a meth dealer, and twenty as an addict, living in a state of bitterness that, in his view, the country had punished him for what they trained and instructed him to do. The elusive "final confessions" to his children were at some point intended to answer the question of who killed John F. Kennedy, and one of his sons has reason to believe, entirely unfounded by hard and public evidence, that the deed was perpetrated by his father.

Hunt's overseer at the White House, H.R. Haldeman, died of abdominal cancer in Santa Barbara, in 1993. He served a total of 18 months for his part in the Watergate affair, after which he reestablished himself as a highly successful businessman, dealing mostly in high end real estate. His colleague, John Ehrlichman, outlived him by six years, dying in Atlanta in 1999. He

---

[79] Mark Feldstein, *Watergate Revisited,*

served one and-a-half years for the scandal, after which he worked as an artist and as a prodigious novelist.

G. Gordon Libby, who had worked as an agent for the FBI and the Treasury, served as legal counsel to CREEP, and was codenamed "Gemstone," ultimately served under five months of prison time and was given a large fine. Liddy continued as a popular radio host through 2012, after writing the autobiographical *Will*, in which he claims to have planned the murder of columnist Jack Anderson. At the age of 84, he has not been widely seen or heard in public since 2012.

Of all the Watergate conspirators, there is only one who never broke ranks with the president and never wrote memoirs or anything revealing his personal knowledge of the scandal. John Mitchell was the ultimate Nixon loyalist until his death from a heart attack in 1988. He served 19 months in prison until he was paroled due to a medical condition. On the day of his parole, "he told reporters who gathered to greet him, 'From henceforth, don't call me. I'll call you.' He never called."[80]

The judge in the Watergate trials, John Sirica, died on August 15, 1992 of cardiac arrest. During his professional years, he did not comment extensively on the trial, but in his book, *To Set the Record Straight*, he made it clear that "Nixon should have been indicted after leaving the presidency for his part in the Watergate cover-up."[81]

James McCord, one of the five who directly participated in the burglary of the Democratic National Committee in the Watergate hotel, has remained anonymous to a greater degree of success than many of his colleagues. Entering his 90th year, the White House electronics expert has not been heard from after several of his works as an author were published.

The "evil genius" of the Nixon administration, Charles "Chuck" Colson, died of a brain hemorrhage in 2012. Following the Watergate era, he became an evangelical minister, which included an extensive prison ministry. In 2000, Jeb Bush restored his right to vote.

John Dean, White house Counsel to President Nixon, is an activist and author, taking aim in particular at conservative Republican agendas and key individuals. He promoted the impeachment of George W. Bush for the Iraq War, but following his role in Watergate, he was disbarred and has never practiced law again. When asked why he made no effort to regain his license to practice, he stated that he never wanted to pursue that line of work again, that it was a "been there, done that."

Leon Jaworski, the second Special Prosecutor, was a presidential appointment, but Nixon might have thought better about keeping Archibald Cox after encountering Jaworski's tenacity,

[80] Lawrence Meyer Washington Post, "John Mitchell, Watergate, Dies at 75"

[81] Bart Barnes, Washington Post, "John Sirica, Watergate Judge, Dies", August 15, 1992

gathered in various legal settings around the United States and as a war-time prosecutor in Germany. Jaworski died in 1982 at his ranch in Wimberley, Texas, while chopping wood.

The famous attack-dog Vice President, Spiro Agnew, rebounded from the Watergate experience in short order, reinventing himself in international trader with numerous mansions in far-flung locations. He died in 1998 at the age of 77 from a sudden onset of previously undiscovered leukemia and is buried in Timonium, Maryland. Despite his strained relations with the president, he was invited to Nixon's funeral and attended. The Nixon daughters returned the favor at his death.

Bob Woodward continues to write privately and contribute to the Washington Post, as does his colleague, Carl Bernstein. In June 2012, Woodward and Bernstein collaborated on a retrospective article in memory of the White House answer four days after the break-in: "'Certain elements may try to stretch this beyond what it is.' press secretary Ronald Ziegler scoffed, dismissing the incident as a 'third-rate burglary.'" The pair go on to describe the entire presidency of Richard Nixon as being embodied within the Watergate mentality, implying that the bulk of his term was spent in vicious retaliation against attacks coming from his most oppositional factions: "In the course of his five-and-a-half year presidency,...Nixon launched and managed five successive, overlapping wars - the anti-Vietnam War movement, the news media, the Democrats, the Justice System and finally, against history itself."

This would certainly represent the liberal view of Nixon's legacy, but unanimity in such matters is impossible, especially as the years go by. In specific polling among the American population, not only have Watergate and the administration of Richard Nixon parted ways, despite a universal knowledge that they are inextricably linked at the literal level, but Nixon himself has been compartmentalized as being among the greatest foreign policy presidents in history, and among the most troubling from a standpoint of corruption. in 1976, 63% deemed him to be the most immoral postwar president, yet in 1986, 12% responded that Nixon was one of the greatest presidents, and he is almost always ranked in the top two for international affairs., where the vastly more popular Kennedy is not.

Richard Nixon had only reached the presidency after successfully figuring out ways to reinvent himself, overcoming one professional setback after another during his long political career. A man of considerable intellect and fierce personal determination, he amply demonstrated the potential power of the presidency to act unilaterally within the nation's internal affairs. In that sense, he did Americans a favor through the constitutional and social crisis of Watergate by forcing the following generation to question the balance between the three branches of government, to carefully consider which conditions should allow one branch to take command over another, to monitor the boundaries of support staff, and to expand the debate over government transparency and official privilege. That said, no matter how many times people point out that he "opened China", Nixon will always have Watergate as a millstone around his neck, and deservedly so. In 1995, 57% of those polled believed "Nixon's influence on American moral values to be negative."[82]

Nixon's Resignation Speech

"Good evening.

This is the 37th time I have spoken to you from this office, where so many decisions have been made that shaped the history of this Nation. Each time I have done so to discuss with you some matter that I believe affected the national interest.

In all the decisions I have made in my public life, I have always tried to do what was best for the Nation. Throughout the long and difficult period of Watergate, I have felt it was my duty to persevere, to make every possible effort to complete the term of office to which you elected me.

In the past few days, however, it has become evident to me that I no longer have a strong enough political base in the Congress to justify continuing that effort. As long as there was such a base, I felt strongly that it was necessary to see the constitutional process through to its conclusion, that to do otherwise would be unfaithful to the spirit of that deliberately difficult process and a dangerously destabilizing precedent for the future.

But with the disappearance of that base, I now believe that the constitutional purpose has been served, and there is no longer a need for the process to be prolonged.

I would have preferred to carry through to the finish whatever the personal agony it would have involved, and my family unanimously urged me to do so. But the interest of the Nation must always come before any personal considerations.

From the discussions I have had with Congressional and other leaders, I have concluded that because of the Watergate matter I might not have the support of the Congress that I would consider necessary to back the very difficult decisions and carry out the duties of this office in the way the interests of the Nation would require.

I have never been a quitter. To leave office before my term is completed is abhorrent to every instinct in my body. But as President, I must put the interest of America first. America needs a full-time President and a full-time Congress, particularly at this time with problems we face at home and abroad.

To continue to fight through the months ahead for my personal vindication would almost totally absorb the time and attention of both the President and the Congress in a period when our entire focus should be on the great issues of peace abroad and prosperity without inflation at

---

[82] Nixon Postmortem, *Annals of the American Academy of Political and Social Science.* Vol. 560 No. 1988, p. 98

home.

Therefore, I shall resign the Presidency effective at noon tomorrow. Vice President Ford will be sworn in as President at that hour in this office.

As I recall the high hopes for America with which we began this second term, I feel a great sadness that I will not be here in this office working on your behalf to achieve those hopes in the next 21/2 years. But in turning over direction of the Government to Vice President Ford, I know, as I told the Nation when I nominated him for that office 10 months ago, that the leadership of America will be in good hands.

In passing this office to the Vice President, I also do so with the profound sense of the weight of responsibility that will fall on his shoulders tomorrow and, therefore, of the understanding, the patience, the cooperation he will need from all Americans.

As he assumes that responsibility, he will deserve the help and the support of all of us. As we look to the future, the first essential is to begin healing the wounds of this Nation, to put the bitterness and divisions of the recent past behind us, and to rediscover those shared ideals that lie at the heart of our strength and unity as a great and as a free people.

By taking this action, I hope that I will have hastened the start of that process of healing which is so desperately needed in America.

I regret deeply any injuries that may have been done in the course of the events that led to this decision. I would say only that if some of my Judgments were wrong, and some were wrong, they were made in what I believed at the time to be the best interest of the Nation.

To those who have stood with me during these past difficult months, to my family, my friends, to many others who joined in supporting my cause because they believed it was right, I will be eternally grateful for your support.

And to those who have not felt able to give me your support, let me say I leave with no bitterness toward those who have opposed me, because all of us, in the final analysis, have been concerned with the good of the country, however our judgments might differ.

So, let us all now join together in affirming that common commitment and in helping our new President succeed for the benefit of all Americans.

I shall leave this office with regret at not completing my term, but with gratitude for the privilege of serving as your President for the past 51/2 years. These years have been a momentous time in the history of our Nation and the world. They have been a time of achievement in which we can all be proud, achievements that represent the shared efforts of the Administration, the Congress, and the people.

But the challenges ahead are equally great, and they, too, will require the support and the efforts of the Congress and the people working in cooperation with the new Administration.

We have ended America's longest war, but in the work of securing a lasting peace in the world, the goals ahead are even more far-reaching and more difficult. We must complete a structure of peace so that it will be said of this generation, our generation of Americans, by the people of all nations, not only that we ended one war but that we prevented future wars.

We have unlocked the doors that for a quarter of a century stood between the United States and the People's Republic of China.

We must now ensure that the one quarter of the world's people who live in the People's Republic of China will be and remain not our enemies but our friends.

In the Middle East, 100 million people in the Arab countries, many of whom have considered us their enemy for nearly 20 years, now look on us as their friends. We must continue to build on that friendship so that peace can settle at last over the Middle East and so that the cradle of civilization will not become its grave.

Together with the Soviet Union we have made the crucial breakthroughs that have begun the process of limiting nuclear arms. But we must set as our goal not just limiting but reducing and finally destroying these terrible weapons so that they cannot destroy civilization and so that the threat of nuclear war will no longer hang over the world and the people.

We have opened the new relation with the Soviet Union. We must continue to develop and expand that new relationship so that the two strongest nations of the world will live together in cooperation rather than confrontation.

Around the world, in Asia, in Africa, in Latin America, in the Middle East, there are millions of people who live in terrible poverty, even starvation. We must keep as our goal turning away from production for war and expanding production for peace so that people everywhere on this earth can at last look forward in their children's time, if not in our own time, to having the necessities for a decent life.

Here in America, we are fortunate that most of our people have not only the blessings of liberty but also the means to live full and good and, by the world's standards, even abundant lives. We must press on, however, toward a goal of not only more and better jobs but of full opportunity for every American and of what we are striving so hard right now to achieve, prosperity without inflation.

For more than a quarter of a century in public life I have shared in the turbulent history of this era. I have fought for what I believed in. I have tried to the best of my ability to discharge those duties and meet those responsibilities that were entrusted to me.

Sometimes I have succeeded and sometimes I have failed, but always I have taken heart from what Theodore Roosevelt once said about the man in the arena, "whose face is marred by dust and sweat and blood, who strives valiantly, who errs and comes short again and again because there is not effort without error and shortcoming, but who does actually strive to do the deed, who knows the great enthusiasms, the great devotions, who spends himself in a worthy cause, who at the best knows in the end the triumphs of high achievements and who at the worst, if he fails, at least fails while daring greatly."

I pledge to you tonight that as long as I have a breath of life in my body, I shall continue in that spirit. I shall continue to work for the great causes to which I have been dedicated throughout my years as a Congressman, a Senator, a Vice President, and President, the cause of peace not just for America but among all nations, prosperity, justice, and opportunity for all of our people.

There is one cause above all to which I have been devoted and to which I shall always be devoted for as long as I live.

When I first took the oath of office as President 51/2 years ago, I made this sacred commitment, to "consecrate my office, my energies, and all the wisdom I can summon to the cause of peace among nations."

I have done my very best in all the days since to be true to that pledge. As a result of these efforts, I am confident that the world is a safer place today, not only for the people of America but for the people of all nations, and that all of our children have a better chance than before of living in peace rather than dying in war.

This, more than anything, is what I hoped to achieve when I sought the Presidency. This, more than anything, is what I hope will be my legacy to you, to our country, as I leave the Presidency.

To have served in this office is to have felt a very personal sense of kinship with each and every American. In leaving it, I do so with this prayer: May God's grace be with you in all the days ahead."

Bibliography

American Political Buttons: *Election of 1960* - www.americanpoliticalbuttons.com

American Presidents Blog - *Richard Nixon vs. Helen Gahagan Douglas,* Nov. 14, 2008 - www.americanpresidents.org

Balfour, Nancy, "President Nixon's Second Term", in *The World Today,* Vol. 29 No. 3, March '73

Biography.com, *Richard Nixon Biography* - www.bioghraphy.com/people.richard-nion-

9424076?=2

Colodny, Len, Gettlin, *Silent Coup, The Removal of a President*, St. Martin's Press: New York, 1991

Epstein, Edward Jay, *Agency of Fear, Part II: The Politics of Law and Order, the Education of Richard Nixon* - www.agencyoffear.com

Feran, Tom - "Eisenhower and Nixon: Two Terms, but not much Endearment" - Cleveland.com, February 19, 2013

Fowler, Greg, "Jerry Voorhis, '48 Nixon Foe", in *The New York Times*, September 12, 1984

Frank, Jeffrey, Dwight Eisenhower and Richard Nixon: The Odd Couple", in *The Economist*, February 2, 2013

Glass, Andrew, "Nixon and Khrushchev Hold Kitchen Debate", in *Politico*, July, 2007

JFK and Nixon - mu.edu - www.mccadams.posc.mu.edu/progjfk1.htm

Kallina, Edmund F., "Was the 1960 Election Stolen? The Case of Illinois", in *Presidential Studies Quarterly*, Vol. 15 No. 1, Winter, 1985

Los Angeles Times, *Looking Back at the 1962 Gubernatorial Race - Debate: Former Governor Edmund G. (Pat) Brown and ex-president's campaign manager discuss the election at Richard Nixon Library and Birthplace.* - March 22, 1992

Matthews, Christopher, *Former Governor Calls Nixon 'Psycho* - SFGate

Mary Ferrell Foundation - *Kennedy/Nixon Debates* - www.maryferrell.org

Mason, Robert "Richard Nixon as Party Leader , '69 - '73: I Was Going to Build a New Republican Party and a New Majority, '69-'73", in *Journal of American Studies, British Association for American Studies 50th Anniversary*. Dec. 2005

Mazlish, Bruce, "Toward a Psychohistorical Inquiry: The Real Richard Nixon", in *The Journal of Interdisciplinary History*, Vol. 1, no. 1, Autumn, 1970

McLaughlin, Dan, *The Southern Strategy and the Lost Majority: How the Republicans Really Lost the South,* Red State, January 11, 2014

Miller Center - *Richard M. Nixon* - www.millercenter.org

Mitchell, Greg, "When a Woman Dared to Run for the U.S. Senate: Helen Gahagan Douglas vs. Richard Nixon", in *The Nation*, July 27, 2012

National Archives and Records Administration - www.archives.gov

Nixon Presidential Library and Museum - www.nixonarchives.com

PBS.org - *Nixon, Early Career* - www.pbs.org

Scobie, Ingrid Winther, "Helen Gahagan Douglas: Broadway Star as Politician", in *California History*, Vol. 66 no. 4, Dec. 12, 1987

Taylor, John H., *Eisenhower and the 1960 Election*, The New Nixon, September 23, 2008

United States Senate Records

U.S. News Opinion - "Eisenhower and Nixon: Secrets of an Unlikely Pair" - www.usnews.com

Watergateinfo/Resignation - *President Richard Nixon's Resignation - Watergate*, www.watergate.info

CPSIA information can be obtained
at www.ICGtesting.com
Printed in the USA
LVHW01s0341261217
560807LV00038B/3103/P